Jesse

Are You A David?

America's Last Hope Volume II

Sheriff Mack

By

Sheriff Richard Mack, Ret.

Cover photo: Constitutional Sheriff Pamela Elliot, Edwards County, Texas
Cover design: Andrew Mezzullo & Kelly Van Shaar
Front cover painting: "David gegen Goliath" by Gebhard Fugel (c. 1900)
Rear cover painting: "David und Goliath" by Osmar Schindler (c. 1888)

Printed in the United States of America by MC Printing, Provo, Utah

First Edition

ISBN: 978-0-9848856-1-9

Edited and typeset by Kelly Van Shaar
www.kellyvanshaar.com

To order books or schedule Richard Mack to speak at an upcoming event, please contact him:

www.CSPOA.org
602-268-9268
P.O. Box 567, Higley, AZ 85236

Dedication

This book is dedicated to my 12 grandchildren: Liberty, Jayni, Jaxson, Ashtyn, Mackenna, Crew, Tyce, Justin, Milly, Jaden, (the two on the way), and to all public servants who have pledged their lives, their fortunes, and their sacred honor, to keep my grandchildren free!

Preface

When I published *The County Sheriff: America's Last Hope* in February of 2009, I hoped that a few of our nation's sheriffs, peace officers, and other local officials would read it and be positively influenced. I knew that most of the public servants who had sworn an oath to uphold and defend the United States Constitution had not read it or did not understand it, just as I hadn't when I first took the oath as a new police officer. If I could get just a few of them to consider the principles of federalism and state sovereignty that resulted in the formation of our Constitution and incorporate these ideals into the way they fulfilled their various offices, it would be worth it.

That book was based on my experiences spanning several decades and represents my own sincere look at America. The resulting melancholy I felt (especially during elections) and my desire to do something to make things better were my primary motivations for writing it. Now, after 100,000 copies have been sold and distributed nationwide I think we can safely say the book has exceeded everyone's wildest expectations; it certainly has mine!

In spite of our occasional victories, however, this time is unprecedented in American history. America's demise is imminent and the need for restoration is a national emergency. A lot has happened in the last five years to make this second book necessary. It's truly amazing: the people I've met, the places I've been and the things I've experienced since writing that book. Thus, my desire to share some of that with you in this sequel. I'd also like to tell you some of the lame-brained excuses I've heard from sheriffs and others for NOT standing up when they should have. If some of what I have to say here makes them a little hot under the collar, so be it!

In the first book I addressed the "gradual and silent" encroachments that Madison warned us about. However, the incremental (Fabianistic) destruction of America and the "fundamental transformation" as promised by Mr. Obama, are no longer silent nor gradual. They are bold and in-your-face, an audacious devastation with a blatant scheme to replace our Constitution with Marxism. (Mr. Obama is certainly not alone in this movement!) That which we fought several wars – including two World Wars – to prevent, which we sacrificed the lives of hundreds of thousands of our nation's soldiers to avoid, we now embrace as common and routine, couched within our contemporary ideals of political correctness!

In the first book I spoke of a $9,000,000,000,000 (trillion) federal debt. Ah! What a joke! It has now doubled! Can you believe we tax, borrow, and spend even more now than we did five years ago? We now borrow **$4.5 billion every day** and spend **$10 billion every day!** And yet we still turn a blind eye and re-elect the criminals responsible for it!

Are we disposed to be of the number of those who having eyes, see not, and having ears, hear not, the things which so nearly concern their temporal salvation?

~ Patrick Henry

We have eyes, but we see not! Why? What is it that keeps us going along with this catastrophic destruction?

On the surface, much of what we see in America seems to be better than ever. Greater technology, advances in the medical field, increased ease of travel and communications, nice cars and smooth freeways, more time and options for entertainment and recreation. Yet many of us understand that the party is almost over. Americans who are paying attention know that today's tyranny, government abuses, corruption, inflated fiat currency, overflowing prisons, disdain for the Constitution, gluttonous debt and mass psychosis spell doom for this once free country. This is the most critical time in our nation's history since the Civil War.

It was the best of times, it was the worst of times, it was the age of wisdom, it was the age of foolishness, it was the epoch of belief, it was the epoch of incredulity, it was the season of Light, it was the

season of Darkness, it was the spring of hope, it was the winter of despair, we had everything before us, we had nothing before us...

~ **Charles Dickens, A Tale Of Two Cities**

The American people are desperately searching for solutions. They want assurances that government officials will be honest, fair, reasonable and actually keep their word to obey the law and defend the Constitution. They want to believe what past generations have taken for granted: that the government exists to serve them and protect their rights!

Courageous leaders with their eyes wide open are our rays of hope in this fast-approaching night, and some sheriffs, chiefs of police, peace officers, county commissioners, city councils, state legislatures, and governors are standing up. Just when we began to despair, state and local officials have made moves to nullify unconstitutional acts of the Federal Government. It appears that there is hope – real hope, not 'campaign jive' hope – to restore liberty in America. If we can accomplish this, future generations may indeed look back on our day as "the best of times."

Has the time come to stand for liberty? You, yes you; the city councilman in Duluth, Georgia, or you, the county commissioner in Graham County, Arizona, or you, the Sheriff in Ravalli County, Montana, or you, the Chief of police in Tomball, Texas, or even you, the patrol officer in St. Charles, Missouri; is it time to stand for liberty? If you believe it's not, then can you please tell us what in the world it would take to change your mind?

I readily admit that the information and principles herein are not mine. I did not make this stuff up; but I did discover it for myself. Now, I am merely the messenger trying to sound the clarion call and help others along that same journey. I hope some will hear; I hope some will educate themselves, begin to see what is really going on and *do something about it!*

It is time to see, it is time to know, and more importantly, *it is time to do!* It is time to do something about the destruction of our country, our liberty, and our Constitution. We can and we must while there is still time. This second book in *America's Last Hope* series will show how we can, and show how the work has already commenced.

One of the most amazing books that has come out during the past few years is entitled *They Fired The First Shot*, authored by "A Friend of Medjugorje." In this masterpiece, the author points the finger right where it should be; at an out of control government doing precisely the opposite of what it should do. The book bravely draws some startling and irrefutable comparisons between Barack Obama and Adolph Hitler. More importantly, perhaps, the author brings home the idea that modern day Davids – sheriffs and other local public servants – are the only viable solution for the restoration of our God-given rights, in conjunction with our willingness to repent and return to God's law as a people. It is from that work that I derive the title for this sequel.

Richard Mack | *Are You A David?*

Introduction

A quick review of 1 Samuel Ch 17, the story of David and Goliath, goes something like this:

> **And there went out a champion out of the camp of the Philistines, named Goliath.**
>
> **And Goliath stood before the Israelite army and said, "Choose ye a man and let him come down to me. If he be able to fight with me, and to kill me, then will we be your servants: but if I prevail against him, and kill him, then shall ye be our servants, and serve us."**
>
> **When Saul and all Israel heard those words of the Philistine, they were dismayed, and greatly afraid.**

And David said to Saul, "I will go and fight this Philistine, I have smote the lion and the bear and this Philistine will be as one of them. The Lord that delivered me out of the paw of the lion, and out of the paw of the bear, he will deliver me out of the hand of this Philistine. "

And David chose five smooth stones from the brook and drew near to the Philistine. And Goliath saw David and disdained him, for he was but a youth. And David took a stone and slang it, and it smote the Philistine in his forehead and he fell to the earth. Therefore, David stood upon the Philistine and slew him with his own sword.

And when the Philistine army saw their champion dead, they fled.

There are many parallels that could be drawn between the biblical story of David and what is going on in America today. However, first and foremost, this book and its author will never advocate violence of any kind, but will indeed advocate standing against the beast, today's Goliath, the real threat, and recognizing the real enemy, just as courageously as David did. Most assuredly, this book supports the humility and valor of young David and his faith in answering the call to defend his country. Are You A David? Will you answer the call?

Of course, "Davids" do not normally win. Usually the biggest and the strongest win and such victors attempt to convince us all that the victory alone makes them right and worthy of admiration. You know, the old "might makes right" cliché. (Something we see frequently in government and politics.)

But winning means *you won;* it doesn't make you morally correct or superior. Being wealthy and powerful does not make you anything special. If it did then the heads of the world's drug cartels would be at the top of the list, but alas, they are nothing but common street thugs, crooks and murderers (albeit wealthy ones). Lamentably, they are not much different from many of our debased politicians: power brokers in DC and our State capitals who sell their birthrights, our nation, and the liberty of the people for power!

David certainly demonstrated what one person can do to make a difference. Now just imagine if we had hundreds, maybe even thousands of Davids today, standing firm against the Goliath-sized threats to the American people and our liberties. There would be no stopping us! We could return to those basic and fundamental principles that America was founded upon and once again make her the constitutional republic she was meant to be. Moreover, the process could and would remain peaceful as our "Davids" stood and interposed themselves, yes, put themselves in the way and on the line for the sake of all Americans!

You will also note that David did not act cocky and did not respond to Goliath's disdain with trash talk or insults. In fact, he remained humble and focused on the task at hand. Goliath, on the other hand, stood before the Israelites and attempted to intimidate them. He wanted them all to be in awe, to be afraid, and to believe that standing against him would be futile. Just as many today say things like, "The Federal

Government is too big; they have all the money, they have all the lawyers, they are invincible," or "You can't fight city hall!" (Who wants you to believe that?)

Remember that Saul had a huge army with the very best in armor and weaponry, and they'd all been camped out for weeks listening to Goliath's taunts and waiting for someone brave enough to accept his challenge. These men no doubt knew that their cause was just, that they were fighting for their families and freedom. But did they stand up to face Goliath? No, not one.

Do you have the faith and courage to take on today's Goliaths? Granted, it is much easier and safer to make nice with him and to continue taking his money. But if we are to change America, we must stand against the powers that are destroying her.

We will never be destroyed from an outside enemy. If we falter and lose our freedoms it will be because we destroyed ourselves.

~ Abraham Lincoln

Thus the need to 1) recognize the real threat and 2) do something about it!

Do the people in your town have someone to turn to when their liberty is threatened? Are you one of the thousands of men in Saul's army 'just following orders' or are you something more?

Are you a David?

The question is not meant to be rhetorical. I hope you ask yourself that question and answer affirmatively each time you look in the mirror; each time you look your constituents in the eye and ask for their vote. They have a right to know! Answer boldly and without hesitation; answer proudly and publicly. Make it known to all federal agencies and politicians that you *are* a David; that you will follow the U.S. Constitution and will not tolerate violation of it in your jurisdiction!

Many others in your position may not heed the call, but that's entirely irrelevant. Standing up when everybody else is standing up, well, that's just polite. Will you answer the call as did David of old? David was a mere shepherd boy; not a seasoned soldier. He was young and humble, yet confident, obedient, courageous, and most importantly, filled with faith.

Make no mistake about this book's intent; we will not restore America unless we first restore ourselves and our families as children of "Nature's God," as stated by the Founders.

Our Constitution was made only for a moral and religious people. It is wholly inadequate to the government of any other.

~ John Adams, Founding Father and second president of the United States

If we do not get ourselves right with the Creator, it makes little difference what else we do. David did not do it without Him and we cannot do so now.

Dr. Martin Luther King stated frequently that we have a moral responsibility to obey *just laws*. However, we likewise have a duty and moral responsibility to disobey *unjust* laws. Nevertheless, many politicians, police officers and even some sheriffs claim there is some higher moral ground in enforcing *unjust* laws until some court rules that the law is unconstitutional. Do they think it's their patriotic duty to go along with unjust laws, abuse and victimize citizens, commit plunder and mayhem until a judge tells them to cease such behavior? Why don't we do it the other way around? Should we not make our own determination as to what is just and unjust? If all laws are to be enforced by our nation's police then how are we any different than Nazi Germany, Red China, or any other communist totalitarian regime? Who is it that has convinced us that doing such is right, correct, ethical or moral? Truly, anyone who subscribes to this backward justification has lost their moral compass.

The upcoming chapters will answer the questions of who is, who should be, and why there are not more *modern day Davids*. It will also prove that the principles of state sovereignty, local autonomy, and the implementation and enforcement of the Tenth Amendment, are indeed the solution for slaying the enemy of Liberty today. We can and we must take America back county by county and state by state. It's the only solution left. If we do not make use of it, Goliath will most assuredly win!

Chapter 1
Three Foundational Principles

Before we explore the solution and convince anyone of its efficacy, we have to know three things. Every student in middle school, high school or college and of course *each and every public servant* should know these three foundational principles of American history. If you claim to love America and attempt to defend her or serve her people without this knowledge you will lose your way.

Principle 1: The purpose of American government is to secure life, liberty, and the pursuit of happiness (ownership of property).

Why do we have government and what do we need it for?

Why do we have police, sheriffs, governors, city councils, school boards, dog catchers, senators, county commissioners, armies, etc.? Specifically, where do we see the legal definition and purpose of all American government? Is it detailed within the Preamble? Perhaps some of the ideals and philosophies are there, but they are generalities. For instance, when the Preamble calls for a "more perfect union" it is a very general reflection on a hoped-for result. The Preamble's reference to "promote the general welfare," is not suggesting that we therefore must create a welfare state and provide for the specific financial stability of each and every citizen. The Preamble is an overall introduction to the purpose of our Constitution. It is beautiful and meaningful, but it does not specify the purpose of American government. However, the Declaration of Independence absolutely does:

"We hold these truths to be self-evident, that all men are created equal, that we are endowed by our Creator, with certain unalienable (un a **lien** able, describing something that cannot have a *lien* placed on it) Rights, that among these are **Life, Liberty,** and the **Pursuit of Happiness.**"

Do we even get this? We can place no liens, take no action whatsoever, to interfere with these **Creator-endowed rights.** These are rights that, according to the beliefs of our Founders, God granted us. Therefore, we had them before our government existed and before the formation of our Constitution or the Bill of Rights. They were gifts from Almighty God!

So, if our rights come from God, why do we need government? Well, the answer is the very next line: "That to secure these rights, Governments are instituted among men..." That almost sounds religious, doesn't it? That's because it is. Could there be a higher calling than that of public servants "securing" God's most precious gifts to His children of **Life,** and **Liberty,** and the opportunity to **pursue happiness?**

Therefore, the purpose of American government – city, county, state, and federal – is to do one thing absolutely and without any ambiguity: **protect, secure, defend, and preserve** the innate God-given rights of each and every individual. If government officials are doing anything else, they are acting outside their proscribed authority, stewardship and purpose. Quite honestly, there is a great deal of government implementing and promoting laws that are entirely antithetical to "securing these rights" and that is precisely what is destroying America today. This is what Reagan referred to when he said,

"Government is not the solution to the problem, government is the problem!"

Note that government exists to protect Life, Liberty and the *pursuit of* happiness. Government has no authorization or responsibility to guarantee or force happiness, only the requirement to *protect* our right to pursue it. The definition of happiness and the actual pursuit of it must be left to the individual or the entire principle of liberty is subverted. However, based on previous drafts of the Declaration and other documents of the period it is clear that the pursuit of happiness was meant to include the right to one's self and one's own property and possessions. This was later stated explicitly in the fourth amendment.

Principle 2: The purpose of the Constitution is to establish and preserve a governmental structure that contains parameters to protect individual rights by promulgating strict *limitations* on government as it fulfills its purpose.

The Constitution was created by the Founders to insure that the aforementioned God-given rights were protected within a system of extremely strict rules and limitations. These people knew well the abuses of a government with too much power, having suffered under the rule of King George III for many years. If the new federal government were allowed carte blanche then individual rights and liberty would always be in peril. So, the Founders focused on a set of rules (supreme laws) that would keep the federal government small, impotent and limited in its scope and breadth.

Thomas Jefferson said the Constitution would be the chains by which all politicians would be bound! In other words, keep them from mischief by the constraints of constitutional law, the supreme law of the land.

As Justice Scalia said in Mack/Printz v US, "...the Constitution's conferral upon Congress of not all governmental powers, but only discrete enumerated ones." (Article1, Section 8 of the Constitution is where we read a list of these enumerated and discrete powers.) Thus, the Constitution equates to **L-I-M-I-T-A-T-I-O-N-S on G-O-V-E-R-N-M-E-N-T!** The entire Constitution "delegates" (the actual terminology used in the Tenth Amendment) 30 powers to the Federal Government. If they want more they must, by law, go through the States or the People.

Principle 3: The purpose of the Bill of Rights is to list specifically certain innate and immutable rights that the government shall not infringe.

The Bill of Rights did not exist until two years after the Constitution was adopted, signed, and approved by the States. (Remember, the States did all this; *they* formed the federal government, and "delegated" to it "discrete and enumerated" assignments.) Several Founders did not approve of the Constitution because it was not strict enough on government and did not contain a specific declaration of rights. So, to prevent any misunderstanding or misconstruction, the Bill of Rights was added to the Constitution on December 15, 1791.

The intent was to show a list of basic, fundamental God-given rights that government could never even think about infringing or legislating against. The Bill of Rights was to be the list of **U-N-T-O-U-C-H-A-B-L-E-S**! (Ironic isn't it, that the one of these ten "untouchables" that uses the phrase **"shall not be infringed"** is the most infringed of them all.)

And here is the quiz at the end of the chapter. Here are the three fundamental questions that all Americans should know the answer to as well as they know their own names:

What is the purpose of all American government?
What is the purpose of the U.S. Constitution?
What is the purpose of the Bill of Rights?

Richard Mack | *Are You A David?*

Chapter 2
The Tea Party

On December 16, 1773, "radicals" and "extremists" converged on the harbor in Marlborough, Massachusetts, and dumped 342 crates of tea from three British ships into the ocean. The protest was a response to the tyranny and oppressive taxation from the British empire. The colonists believed that a free people should not be subject to the whims of a King and that their religious beliefs required them to defy tyranny. That tea dumping event is known as the Boston Tea Party.

On April 19, 1775, Paul Revere left Charlestown, Massachusetts to Concord and Lexington to warn Samuel Adams, John Hancock, and other Sons of Liberty that the

Redcoats (British soldiers) were coming to arrest them and confiscate their firearms. (This is a prime example of why the Founders included the Second Amendment in the Bill of Rights some 15 years later; they knew tyrants preferred an unarmed citizenry.) Captain John Parker, the commander of the American Militia (citizen volunteers), ordered his fellow Patriots to not fire unless the Redcoats fired first. "But if they want a war," Parker shouted, "let it begin here." And it did!

On July 4, 1776, Thomas Jefferson and John Dickinson presented their Declaration of Independence to 55 merchants, farmers, doctors, lawyers, and other state delegates all representing the thirteen original States, mutually pledging "our lives, our fortunes, and our sacred honor" to the Holy Cause of Liberty. The signers of this declaration all essentially signed their own death warrants and immediately put themselves under condemnation of the British crown. Each were now considered traitors and criminals of the utmost kind. Indeed, some died horrible deaths along with their families at the hands of the Redcoats.

But these men loved liberty, America, and their fellow man. They risked all to be free, standing firm in their belief that defiance of tyranny was obedience to God! They persevered despite overwhelming odds. Their victory over the greatest military force in the world was nothing short of a miracle. A true parallel to the story of David vs Goliath, and yet today we are turning our backs on all they did, all they believed, and all they fought and died for.

There is a new Tea Party movement blossoming with great vigor and zeal in America, and the vivid similarities between the abuses of King George III and the current state of affairs makes it easy to see why the organizers have chosen that particular name. Mr. Obama and his willing band of thugs caused the contemporary Tea Parties just as King George III caused the original Tea Party in 1773. Many in positions of power try to accuse the Tea Party members of being racists and bigots. The truth of the matter is that the ire aimed at Obama has nothing to do with his heritage or the color of his skin. It is simply a result of his obvious and blatant disdain for American ideals and the U.S. Constitution.

One glaring example of such tyranny is Obama's own pet project, the Affordable Care Act. Ask yourself a little question: How does nationalized socialistic health care forced onto Americans square with individual liberty and the principles of limited government? Should you be able to choose for yourself the type of health care you want or should it be shoved down your throat by government agents? Yes, the thugs in our government are in charge of enforcing Obamacare, and the IRS will make certain we are all in compliance!

Forced government health care by IRS agents who are there to follow the orders of a dictatorial executive in Washington DC! Yes, this "Affordable" health care act *may* provide some medical benefits to some people in our nation, but at what cost? One of the many costs will be that of personal choice and the loss of the constitutional republic we once revered as sacred. Now we surrender it all for programs, entitlements and politics. America is dying, but for the first time in American history we have provided health care benefits to the needy among us! A price our leaders are all too willing to force us to pay! Is there any way to stop this? Is there a way we can save America?

Richard Mack | *Are You A David?*

Chapter 3
The Solution

The sad truth about our current predicament is that our options are extremely limited. The place you can pretty much forget about pursuing any solution is in Washington DC. You will not find a track record there which shows any attempt to restore or secure the most remote semblance of liberty. What you will find in DC is corruption, treason, taxation, spending, borrowing, unsustainable debt, and passing laws to pay back the campaign donations electees received from huge corporations! Who can protect us from such lawlessness and criminality? Is there anyone assigned to defend Americans against criminals in government? Do local officials have a moral and legal obligation to keep their oaths of allegiance to the Constitution and at the same time support all politicians who don't? Is there a solution?

Yes, we could all dream and wish that Washington DC insiders will stop their own abuse, tyranny, and crimes. But we know better, and so did the Founders. In fact, they planned for it.

> **We can safely rely on state legislatures to erect the barriers against the encroachments of the national authority.**
>
> **~ James Madison**

Erecting these barriers is the answer! This solution is also made clear in several recent U.S. Supreme Court rulings, one in particular when two sheriffs sued the Clinton administration in 1994. Some excerpts from this ruling are listed below to reinforce the principles we are considering here. It deserves repeating that a couple of sheriffs sued the federal government and won a landmark decision on the issue of state sovereignty and the Tenth Amendment, the ruling having been released on June 27, 1997. Does your sheriff know about this landmark case? More importantly, will your sheriff enforce the principles as contained within this ruling?

> **We have held however, that state legislatures are not subject to federal direction.**

(Don't you wish that your local legislators knew this? Perhaps we should make our DC legislators aware of this, as well.)

> **The Federal Government, we held, may not compel the States to enact or administer a federal**

regulatory program.

What does this do to Obamacare? Is there any way we could interpret Obamacare as not qualifying as "a federal regulatory program?" Is there any reason the states should 1) Administer this program for or with the federal government or 2) Allow the federal government to come into the state and force it upon our citizens against their will?

...They [the States] retained an inviolable sovereignty.

In other words, the States do not answer to Congress or the President, and they certainly do not answer to federal bureaucracies!

Residual State Sovereignty was also implicit of course, in the Constitution's conferral upon Congress of not all governmental powers, but only discrete enumerated ones, which implication was *rendered express* by the Tenth Amendment's assertion...

In other words, the Tenth Amendment must be **a-s-s-e-r-t-e-d** if we are going to safeguard state sovereignty and keep the federal government within its proscribed "discrete and enumerated powers." To keep them impotent and off our backs we must "erect the barriers" and assert the Tenth Amendment!

The Constitution thus contemplates that a State's government will represent and remain accountable to its own citizens.

States are not accountable or answerable to the federal government, but to the people! If state and local officers acquiesce and accept bribes or grants from the feds and in turn do whatever it takes to keep the money flowing in, then we lose a vital part of personal liberty.

...One of the Constitution's structural protections of liberty.

What is a "structural protection of liberty?" **State sovereignty** is what the U.S. Supreme Court was referring to! Because our duty is to maintain **"a healthy balance of power between the States and the Federal Government."** If we do not then we lose one of our **"Constitution's structural protections of liberty!"**

The only manner in which the "protections of liberty" and a "healthy balance of power" can be maintained is **IF** the people's employees in each city, county, and state, dedicate themselves to the preservation of American exceptionalism as delineated within the Constitution, the Declaration of Independence and the Bill of Rights. (It should be noted here that this solution is the *only* peaceful solution left. The aforementioned "employees" have it within their power to prevent a violent remedy. Achieving such a remedy is absolutely the purpose of this book!)

The power of the Federal Government would be augmented immeasurably if it were able to impress into its service – and at no cost to itself – the police officers of the 50 States.

But, the peace officers of the 50 States can choose to go along, and many do to receive the financial benefits described earlier. Some go along for other reasons though. Some simply believe doing so is good law enforcement business and that working together helps everyone and provides better service to the people. This book makes no assertion that cooperation between federal and local agencies is wrong or unconstitutional. However, when you research what authority the feds lawfully have within counties and cities, and if we were to only work with federal agencies where they have constitutional jurisdiction and authority, then cooperation among the feds and local agencies would be greatly diminished. It is irrefutable that the federal government has some prescribed constitutional law enforcement assignments, but it is likewise irrefutable that such policing assignments are very limited. They are as follows:

1) **Treason**
2) **Counterfeiting**
3) **Piracies and felonies committed on the high seas**
4) **Offenses against the Law of Nations**
5) **Invasion** (protecting our borders!)

If the federal government were authorized by the Supremacy Clause to do whatever it wanted, then why did the Framers of the Constitution feel it necessary to list *five* law enforcement tasks and responsibilities within the United States Constitution, detailing what they were allowed to do?

These five powers are precisely in keeping with the intent of the entire Constitution, to keep the federal government impotent with only "discrete and enumerated powers." Anything that the federal government wants to do outside its enumerated powers must be filtered through the Tenth Amendment's checks and balances, "all powers not delegated to the United States by the Constitution...are reserved to States respectively, or to the people." Thus, state sovereignty is preserved and the liberty of the individual also. Therefore, nullification is vital. Our enemies, through pragmatic incremental legislation, have been nullifying our Constitution and Bill of Rights for decades. Why not fight back in similar fashion? Frankly, anyone attempting to convince you that state nullification is wrong or even illegal does not understand history, the enforcement of the Tenth Amendment, or the principles of state sovereignty. Furthermore, if we are indeed, "not subject to federal direction," then nullification is a natural and common-sense recourse. Are we to leave the States with no options and some sort of mythical obligation to bypass the oath of allegiance to the Constitution and render blind loyalty to those who routinely violate their oaths in Washington DC? What utter nonsense! How can we take an oath, literally swear to obey and defend our constitutions, both State and Federal, and then self-righteously claim a higher moral duty to violate said oath because lawmakers expect us to go along with their payback legislation to donors?

Chapter 4
Excuses

If you do not know yourself and you do not know your enemy, you will lose every battle.

~ Chinese warrior Sun-tzu, 2500 years ago

If sheriffs do not know themselves, do not know their job responsibilities, do not know their own power or from whom it comes and who it is for, and if they do not know the real enemy or from whom the real threat is coming, then how could they ever secure the blessings of liberty?

While the proliferation of the Constitutional Sheriff movement and the Oath Keeper awakening over the last five years has been remarkable, there has also been a great outpouring of excuses from some local "leaders" as to why they will not stand for liberty and against tyranny. The answers at times deserve an 'A' for creativity, but more often than not, are the same mindless drivel from those who lack insight, courage, patriotism and a fundamental grasp of American history. This writing would be remiss if it did not address the concerns and fears of those who could legitimately save our country, but for some reason choose not to.

Everything is backward in America today. Peace officers are taught that they would be doing something wrong if they stood and defended principles of liberty and enforced the Bill of Rights. The truth of the matter is the complete opposite! The cop who stands up is not doing anything wrong or violating any law, but absolutely obeying the law!

Without question, the most overused excuse from sheriffs and other local officials for failing to keep their oaths is the fear they have of losing all the federal "free money." Of course, they don't always call it "free money," but many of them do and even worse, some actually believe it is *free!* The "free money" is actually federal grants, but would more accurately be termed **bribes.** Regardless of what they're called, the proof that these bribes are working is that so many local "leaders" are willing to compromise liberty in order to retain the funding from our most magnanimous and benevolent federal government. This must be a new magnanimous and benevolent federal government, because it certainly is not the old constitutional and lawful federal government! When anyone gives you money they are expecting something in return. They are buying something; your services or favors or at times, your friendly support. It's insurance! If anything ever goes wrong, they know they have someone in their pocket to rely on. For any sheriff to say he is afraid to stand against federal intrusions out of fear of losing federal funds, proves that the "grants" are working just as anticipated by those who dole them out. There never has been and never will be a "free lunch" or "free money." If local leaders expect to receive this money with no strings attached then well, let's just say they are out of touch with reality.

And that leads us to the next excuse. Some sheriffs say "Sheriff Mack is out of touch with modern law enforcement" and therefore is unqualified to give advice or training to anyone. They also say, "Sheriff Mack isn't even a sheriff anymore." Or, "Sheriff Mack is all wet when it comes to the Constitution." Leave Mack out of it. Just look at what's going on. Did the sheriffs in this country listen to Sheriff Mack when he was a sheriff? They did not then any more than they do now!

I readily admit that I am not a sheriff anymore and have not been in law enforcement for over 17 years. I could very well be unfamiliar with the latest techniques for handcuffing a suspect, the state of the art computers utilized in patrol vehicles or any number of other police toys being strapped to an officer's waist that perhaps were not there 17 years ago. I may be "out of touch" with some of that. I definitely am out of touch with the horrifying increase in police brutality plaguing this nation and I am way out of touch with the militarization of our police departments and sheriffs' offices all across this country. I guarantee I could help any police agency decrease the frequency of such problems, but these issues are not my primary topics or banners. Where I am **not** out of touch is with the principles of liberty America was supposed to revere, the oath of office that we were supposed to keep and the true service we are sworn to provide the American people. I am not out of touch with any of those ideals.

Another prevalent excuse is, "The federal government would never do that." Many sheriffs say this and make specific reference to the FBI. Well, you may have some friends in the FBI or some relatives who work for the Bureau, as do we all. However, careful examination of the FBI will expose numerous crimes within that agency. After the Waco fiasco and the killing of 89 men, women, and children, the FBI "investigated" their own handling of the incident. The Davidian compound was set ablaze and the FBI blamed the Davidian leader David Koresh for setting the fire as part of a suicide pact. (Davidian survivors said this never happened) Furthermore, the FBI said they had used no pyrotechnic devices whatsoever, or anything that could have started the fire. Then two years later spent pyrotechnic devices were discovered within FBI evidence lockers that were indeed used at the Waco Davidian compound.

So a new investigation was called for by Congress. The stated goal was to have an "independent" and "thorough" examination of the incident. The result was another Washington DC whitewash as Senator Orrin Hatch oversaw the new Waco report. Nothing happened and the new investigation answered nothing as to why the pyrotechnic devices were used, why the FBI lied about the devices, and why the FBI listed the devices as "miscellaneous evidence" after the first investigation. (We should all be proud of them for not throwing them away.) Numerous crimes had been committed by the FBI including falsifying evidence, perjury, obstruction of justice and conspiracy. No, not one single agent was ever prosecuted.

Then recently during another investigation by congress, a citizen, Becky Gerritson, testified that she tried to form a Tea Party group and submitted an application for 501c3 status from the IRS. She broke down sobbing several times during her testimony as she detailed ruthless harassment and abuse from the IRS and the FBI! It appeared that the IRS asked the FBI to help them harangue and intimidate Ms. Gerritson. Why was all this done? To discourage anyone and everyone from speaking out for liberty, for the Constitution, and against the president!

So, to logically solve all these abuses many leaders tell us to change who we vote for and that if we don't like the things our government does then vote for someone who will change it all for us! Now why didn't the victims of IRS crimes think of this??? All they have to do is vote for somebody else!

When Warren and Shirley Black were ordered to spend one year in Leavenworth for "failing to sign some IRS papers," why didn't their children simply start a national campaign to vote some different politicians into office? This takes us back to the ideal that public servants exist to protect the rights of the individual against the mob. The partisan faithful of both major parties are not going to stop voting for their main players (career politicians) just because a few hundred people got victimized by the IRS. Besides, "everyone should pay their fair share." The best excuse for not helping your neighbor, "They should have paid their fair share. I pay mine."

The victims of government abuse are in no way capable of turning the tide of mainstream politics to obtain redress for the crimes committed against them. To do that from jail or while fighting 25 years in court would make such a political undertaking even more unlikely, if not completely impossible. These victims are actually told by their servants, "Next time pay your taxes or get a better lawyer." What complete and utter calloused arrogance!

And where does that leave, "The federal government would never do that?" Well, it leaves it right where it has always been; as just another excuse with no basis in fact. But you know what they say, "There's no such thing as a bad excuse."

A sheriff in Boise, Idaho, came up with one of the all-time blue ribbon excuses. You gotta love it. Ada County Sheriff Gary Raney, tired of being asked if he would be a Constitutional Sheriff, finally responded publicly that he had taken an oath to support and defend the *"whole"* Constitution, and therefore was under solemn obligation to allow the federal government its rightful reign and power within Ada County as per the Supremacy Clause.

This Constitution, and the Laws of the United States which shall be made in pursuance thereof;... shall be the supreme law of the land; and the judges in every state shall be bound thereby, anything in the constitution or laws of any state to the contrary notwithstanding.

~ The Supremacy Clause (found in Article Six, Clause 2 of the U.S. Constitution)

A couple of problems here. Based on the above, what is the supreme law of the land? Two things: First, **The Constitution**, and second, the laws of the United States (i.e., the Federal Government) made in *pursuance* thereof, (in agreement with), the Constitution. And how do we know if a Federal law is in agreement with the Constitution? Well, to begin with it has to be in one of the very few categories where the Constitution itself says the Feds are allowed to make law, (Some are listed in the previous chapter; the full list is in Article 1, Section 8) Anything outside that very limited scope and it's automatically out. Next, the law has to not do anything that is forbidden by the constitution (such as trample on individual or states' rights.)

When the Supremacy Clause is really understood, it can be a powerful force for good. It takes a real stretch to interpret this as no matter what, the Federal Government is always right, is the boss of everybody and everything, and if you get in their way you're breaking your oath. (Obama has used this propaganda a great deal)

BUT if Sheriff Raney really means it about supporting the *whole* constitution, then why haven't we heard of his constitutional stands for a gold and silver standard in Idaho as required by Article 1, Sec 10, or his advocacy for an Article 5 convention of the States, OR his objections to the Federal Reserve even existing as *only* Congress is allowed to coin money and set the value thereof (Article 1 Section 8). Perhaps this is going out on a limb here, but has Sheriff Raney really made any meaningful stands for the Constitution? Or could it be the **ONLY** stand he has ever made related to the Constitution is his excuse as to why he is *not* enforcing it?

As the dedicated servant of the people of Ada County, he will keep his oath to protect and defend the federal government's authorization to do whatever it wants! How does Raney's philosophy coincide with the Ninth and Tenth Amendments? The Founders actually *went further* in the Bill of Rights to clarify some principles that they did not feel were worded strongly enough in the original Constitution:

> **The enumeration in the Constitution, of certain rights, shall not be construed to deny or disparage others retained by the people.**
>
> **~ Ninth Amendment to the U.S. Constitution**

> **Tenth Amendment: The powers not delegated to the United States by the Constitution, nor prohibited by it to the States, are reserved to the States respectively, or to the people.**
>
> **~ Tenth Amendment to the U.S. Constitution**

One of the ultimate questions for Sheriff Raney and all sheriffs and chiefs of police is this: Would you allow the federal government to conduct door-to-door confiscations of firearms from the people within your jurisdictions?

For crying out loud don't make another excuse! Just answer the question. Would you allow such confiscations in your community? Because many of you already are.

Sheriffs who cling to these excuses foment frustration and

anger among the people and leave the victims alone, scared and desperate. Painting law-abiding citizens into a corner can only lead to tragedies. Such tragedies most definitely can be prevented! If you could prevent them; wouldn't you at least try?

In questions of power, then, let no more be heard of confidence in man, but bind him down from mischief by the chains of the Constitution.

~ Thomas Jefferson

Chains! Sheriff Raney and others like him would seem to disagree with Jefferson, informing us that the Supremacy Clause removes all chains from federal officers, and that, in fact, it negates the Bill of Rights and most of the Constitution and leaves only the parts directed at the States.

And to finish off the chapter, here are a few other excuses we've heard way too often:

Sheriff, will you keep your oath of office? "There is no law saying that I am required to keep the oath of office or how I am required to keep it. Besides, no one keeps their oath these days."

Are you a constitutional sheriff? "I do the best I can and I am as constitutional as the next guy. Anyway, Sheriff Mack does not know the pressures we face here in our county and his book just does not apply that much to us."

Sheriff, will you stand for liberty? "Jurisdiction is a complicated matter. I just don't have the authority to tell the federal government what to do."

Regardless of what excuse people use for not standing up, it all comes out the same: The people are left with no recourse. Remember that there is one law that we must obey even before the Constitution: *God's law,* and standing for liberty in the defense of the defenseless is an integral part of that law.

Moderation in defense of liberty is no virtue.

~ Barry Goldwater

Chapter 5
No Truer Words Ever Spoken

If voting made a difference they wouldn't let us do it! (Mark Twain)

Extremism in defense of liberty is no vice. (Barry Goldwater)

America will never be destroyed from the outside. If we falter and lose our freedoms, it will be because we destroyed ourselves. (Abraham Lincoln)

I don't make jokes. I just watch government and report the facts. (Will Rogers)

We can expect extreme efforts to discredit Mack and his

Message. (Linda Turley-Hansen)

The Constitution is not the problem. It is emphatically the answer. (Shane Krauser)

It is entirely possible to defend yourself from an intruder breaking into your home, but nearly impossible to defend yourself against a criminal government!

Obama spent $700 million to create a $5 million health care website!

A person is judged by how well they honor those to whom a promise was made. (Unknown)

We are fast approaching the stage of the ultimate inversion: the stage where government is free to do anything it pleases, while the citizens may only act by permission. (Ayn Rand)

If you do not know yourself and you do not know your enemy, you will lose every battle. (Sun-tzu, <u>The Art of War</u>)

One of the charges in the articles of impeachment against President Richard Nixon was that he used the IRS to attack and intimidate his political enemies!

It's not yours to give. (Davy Crockett's constituent referring to Congressional spending habits)

We do not need the government's permission to exist, but they in fact, do need our permission to exist. (Michael Badnarik)

Definition of **insanity**: Doing the same thing over and over and expecting a different result. (Albert Einstein)

Insanity is perpetuated with: "That's the way we've always done things."

Socialism is a philosophy of failure, a creed of ignorance, and the gospel of envy, its inherent virtue is the equal sharing of misery. (Winston Churchill)

There is no way you can keep an oath to protect and preserve a document that you have never read!

Under Reagan, 19% of the American people paid no federal income tax, Clinton was 25%, Bush 30% and Obama 47%. (Government Gone Wild)

It's easier for a terrorist (from the Middle East) to enter our country than it is for an American citizen to get on an airplane!

Cowards will continuously find a thousand reasons why they won't do what they are afraid to, yet always criticize those who do!

The only thing you have to do to be labeled a nut, a kook, or a racist, is quote the Founding Fathers. It gets even worse if you recite the Constitution.

Socialism and liberty cannot co-exist. Liberty can only survive when government respects the success and failures of each individual.

The only difference between today's slavery and the slavery of the old South is that at least the plantation owners paid for the chains. (Alan Keyes)

Hitler, Stalin, Mao, and Lenin all depended on local officers to cooperate with their laws of death and destruction. The horrible results were pretty much the same either way!

He who passively accepts evil is as much involved in it as he who helps perpetuate it. (Martin Luther King, Jr.)

Americans spend over 6.6 **billion** hours per year attempting to comply with the complex federal tax code!

Even if the IRS and the federal income tax were lawful, the IRS would never possess the right, the authority, or any lawful legitimacy for monitoring a single citizen's spending habits or personal finances.

No law should ever be more than 50 pages long!

Our leaders care about two things; election and re-election.

Freedom is far more essential to human happiness than safety. (Betty Akers)

We are not in trouble because we are following the Constitution too strictly!

Policies and regulations of federal bureaucracies cannot and do not supersede the Constitution or the Bill of Rights. No matter how many courts or politicians say so, it could never be!

Gun control in America is against the law!

To disarm the people is the best and most effectual way to enslave them. (George Mason)

Stand up for a cause and you will get mowed down. (The Majestic)

What was once unthinkable has now become politically routine.

America is on the exact path as was ancient Rome right before its collapse.

Freedom is defined by the extent to which government leaves you alone; that your choices to help others remain a matter of conscience, not governmental force.

Liberty is for everyone; no excuses, no exceptions, not by anyone, not at any time!

The Democrats and Republicans have completely controlled and monopolized our government at every level for over 100 years.

No one, nowhere, no power can change nature's law. They can only violate it. (*They Fired The First Shot*)

Everyday courage has few witnesses. But yours is no less noble because no drum beats for you and no crowds shout your name. (Robert Louis Stevenson)

Taking our country further in to debt and passing that debt on to our children, "is irresponsible and unpatriotic!" (Senator Barack Obama)

We will never vote ourselves out of this crisis!

When injustice becomes law, resistance becomes duty.

Chapter 6
No Greater Lies Ever Told

The Affordable Care Act is constitutional, because it's a tax! (Justice Roberts)

We're from the government and we're here to help you.

(Regarding the Internal Revenue Service) There's not a smidgen of corruption. (Barack Obama)

I feel your pain. (Bill Clinton)

I accept full responsibility.

It takes a village. (Hillary Clinton)

We can't make any other cuts to federal spending. There's just no place left to make any cuts. (This regarding a U S federal budget that has increased over 500% in the last 25 years!) (Nancy Pelosi)

It's free money!

What difference, at this point, does it make? (Hillary Clinton)

The era of big government is over. (President Clinton)

I have no authority to interfere. (Sheriff Gillespie)

The federal tax system is voluntary. (Senator Harry Reid)

Gun control will make us all safer. (Adolf Hitler)

We were attacked [in the Gulf of Tonkin] (LBJ)

I am not a crook (Nixon)

Read my lips - No New Taxes (GHW Bush)

I did not have sex with that woman, Miss Lewinski (Bill Clinton)

Obama:
- I will have the most transparent administration in history.
- The stimulus will fund shovel-ready jobs.
- I am focused like a laser on creating jobs.

- The IRS is not targeting anyone.
- It was a spontaneous riot about a movie.
- I will put an end to the type of politics that "breeds division, conflict and cynicism".
- You didn't build that!
- I will restore trust in Government.
- The public will have 5 days to look at every bill that lands on my desk
- Whistle blowers will be protected in my administration.
- We got back every dime we used to rescue the banks and auto companies, with interest.
- I am not spying on American citizens.
- ObamaCare will be good for America .
- You can keep your family doctor.
- Premiums will be lowered by $2500.
- If you like it, you can keep your current healthcare plan.
- It's just like shopping at Amazon.
- I knew nothing about "Fast and Furious" gunrunning to Mexican drug cartels.
- I knew nothing about IRS targeting conservative groups.
- I knew nothing about what happened in Benghazi .
- The world is less violent than it has ever been. It is healthier than it has ever been. It is more tolerant than it has ever been. It is better fed than it's ever been. It is more educated than it's ever been.

And the biggest of all Obama's lies:

"I, Barrack Hussein Obama, pledge to preserve, protect and defend the Constitution of the United States of America ."

Chapter 7
EPA = UNCONSTITUTIONAL

The landmark Mack/Printz case of 1997 answered many questions about federalism and State Sovereignty. Indeed, it was arguably the most powerful Tenth Amendment decision in our nation's history. Besides all the principles of "dual sovereignty" as explained by Justice Scalia and the lack of federal authority within "local and municipal" jurisdictions, the Supreme Court makes a rather surprising historical reference regarding the EPA . In this monumental ruling filed by two small-town sheriffs, the succinct historical review by the Court will astonish even the most complacent observer. Scalia quotes the Federalist Papers and Madison frequently in this case, but he also refers to the "prior jurisprudence" of the Supreme Court. In doing so, the Court makes it clear that the

EPA was ruled to be *UNCONSTITUTIONAL* in the early 1970s. Rather than attempt to convince the reader that this actually is the truth, let us simply look at the Mack/Printz decision and quote the U.S. Supreme Court word for word:

Finally, and most conclusively in the present litigation, we turn to the prior jurisprudence of this Court. Federal commandeering of state governments is such a novel phenomenon that this Court's first experience with it did not occur until the 1970s, when the Environmental Protection Agency promulgated regulations requiring States to prescribe auto emissions testing, monitoring and retro-fit programs, and to designate preferential bus and carpool lanes. The Courts of Appeals for the Fourth and Ninth Circuits invalidated the regulations on statutory grounds in order to avoid what they perceived to be grave constitutional issues, see *Maryland v. EPA,*530 F. 2d 215, 226 (CA4 1975); *Brown v. EPA,* 521 F. 2d 827, 838-842 (CA9 1975); and the District of Columbia Circuit invalidated the regulations on both constitutional and statutory grounds, see *District of Columbia v.Train,* 521 F. 2d 971, 994 (CADC 1975). After we granted certiori to review the regulations, the Government declined even to defend them, and instead rescinded some and conceded the invalidity of those that remained, leading us to vacate the opinions below and remand for consideration of mootness. *EPA v. Brown,* 431 U.S. 99 (1971).

Although we had no occasion to pass upon the subject in Brown, later opinions of ours have made clear that the Federal Government may not

compel the States to implement, by legislation or executive action, federal regulatory programs.

Well, glory be! The U.S. Supreme Court telling the feds that their overreaching tactics and regulations are not proper and the government itself "declined even to defend them," referring to their own rules and policies. You are probably wondering then; why do we still have the EPA making their own laws, enforcing all their regulations as if they were judge, jury, and executioner, and acting as if they owned our states and counties? To understand this we must first comprehend the establishment of the bureaucracies that have completely taken over Washington DC and American politics. The easy answer is; we have all gone to sleep and we trusted someone the Founders warned us to never trust; POLITICIANS and BUREAUCRATS!

The EPA now issues fines to citizens without due process; no hearings, no trials, no "innocent until proven guilty" requirements. They do whatever they want to whomever they want and there's very little we can do about it. (Who does the EPA think they are, the IRS?) Even though the States are entirely capable of dealing with clean water and air, and in fact, have their own bureaucracies charged with doing just that, the EPA is now more powerful than ever before, the Brown and Maryland cases notwithstanding. It's easy to circumvent state sovereignty if the media and our local "leaders" allow it. If it's a "good idea" or if it is indeed "for the good of the environment," then get out of the way, our politicians have an agenda to shove down our throats, the Constitution be damned! The EPA is the federal bureaucracy that has destroyed more jobs and property rights than all wars combined!

In the Mack/Printz case SCOTUS offers the solution for such tyranny:

...But the Constitution protects us from our own best intentions. It divides power among sovereigns and among branches of government precisely so that we may resist the temptation to concentrate power in one location as an expedient solution to the crisis of the day.

That phrase, "crisis of the day" is reflective of what seems to be the motto of the Obama administration: "Never let a good crisis go to waste."

Well, it is the same philosophy behind the EPA and all other bureaucracies in DC; they have to form all these agencies to protect our land, forests, rivers, lakes, to stop disease, or drug abuse, and of course, to make sure we all pay our "fair share." But you see, no matter how worthy or benevolent the cause, if it does not coincide with our Constitution, then the government **IS NOT ALLOWED** to do it!

But the Constitution protects us from our own best intentions.

As crazy as it may sound, Arizona can run its own land, air, rivers and lakes, and so can all the other sovereign States! They can even form compacts with neighboring States to keep shared rivers clean and productive for one and all. It would even be a sure wager (on the State approved lottery, of course) that Arizona could run its own education, and even run the Grand Canyon without the interference from our dear

Big DC Brother! The Federal Government is not our boss, and therefore, the EPA is not our boss. They have no law enforcement authority or jurisdiction within the States whatsoever. Local officials, county commissions, sheriffs, and county attorneys should make certain that local citizens are protected from the whimsical regulations of this unbridled DC bureaucracy.

Let's make sure we did not miss anything here;
1) The EPA does not have law enforcement authority.
2) The EPA is not allowed to make it's own laws.
3) The EPA routinely violates the principles of federalism and State Sovereignty.
4) The States can and should run their own geography and natural resources.
5) The States are not subject to Federal direction. (Mack/Printz v US)

The EPA has detroyed more jobs in America than all the recessions and depressions combined. The Environmental Protection Agency is indeed UNCONSTITUTIONAL. Even without the aforementioned evidence, you pretty much know the EPA is out of control and unbridled. But then again, maybe we should just let all this go. They know what's best for us. They're much wiser than Henry, Franklin, Jefferson, Madison, Adams, and Washington! We have to take care of our environment no matter what the Constitution says. What would we have without the Environmental Protection Agency?

FREEDOM, LOGGING, COAL MINING AND A VIBRANT ECONOMY!

Richard Mack | *Are You A David?*

Chapter 8
I Should Have Done More

This latest IRS scandal is just another DC dog and pony show. It has no substance and very little truth. The fact remains that every single one of the members of Congress knows that the IRS has been doing this and much worse for decades. A few of them – including Rand Paul and his father – have been exposing much of it for years. Many will claim, "I didn't know, how could this happen?" Of course, this is the ultimate strategy of one Mr. Obama. Never know anything so you take responsibility for *nothing!* He certainly is not alone!

I too am not without guilt. I readily admit it. I watched as people were attacked by the IRS in my county when I was sheriff. I knew what the IRS was, I witnessed what they did to my own father as they harassed and harangued and stripped him of his dignity, finances, and his faith in the government he had dedicated his life to for 35 years. Yes, in the mid 70s, my father was randomly audited. They concluded that he owed them $6,000. It may as well have been $600,000. We did not have it. We had a three bedroom home, one family car, and sometimes a piece-of-junk car or pickup for us kids to drive around. We were thoroughly middle class and had very little extra.

My dad was innocent of these IRS claims and charges; the unpaid taxes and fines were all a fabrication. He obtained help and tried to work out a solution, but the intimidation increased. So my father fought, he went to hearings and meetings with the IRS agents. He got nowhere, the lies continued. A couple of friends, Rene Richardson (a lawyer) and Lavar Reed (a CPA) came to his aid. Richardson and Reed kept working and discovered the truth; my dad had overpaid his taxes by $600. The IRS owed him! The IRS still did not relent. Finally, my father begged help from Congressman Eldon Rudd, a former FBI agent who had worked with my father as such. Rudd must have done something with the irrefutable evidence Richardson and Reed had discovered, because a week later the IRS told my dad that the matter was resolved and that they would call everything square. Meaning my father had to pay nothing and the IRS would leave him alone. So they left without even an apology after 18 months of torment and hell. Some Americans get this same anguish for 20 years, even more!

Anyway, the IRS never paid my father one dime of the $600 they owed him, but finally, left him alone. Hooray for us! We were now free of this tyrannical nightmare, but our neighbors were not! The IRS did not stop this sort of activity! They merely went on to some other poor unsuspecting sap. They victimized other Americans. Eldon Rudd may have helped my father, but he did not stop the IRS from committing the same crimes against future victims, nor did anyone else in Washington. Why? It's so astonishing, it is so frustrating to see these federal crimes committed and those responsible do nothing about it! Is there a David anywhere?

In 1997, just a few months after I left the Sheriff's Office, I saw congressional hearings about IRS crimes. A few IRS whistle-blowers – yes, IRS agents – testified that the IRS routinely does to thousands of Americans exactly what they had done to my father about 20 years earlier. Jennifer Long was one such whistle-blower and, along with some of her colleagues, pointed out that "If the American people knew what was happening within the IRS there would be a revolution tomorrow." Specifically, these very few courageous federal agents swore in open court that the IRS routinely **fabricated** evidence against law-abiding citizens who the IRS knew could not afford to defend themselves; the exact crime perpetrated against my own father. (And just for the record, the cowards in Congress did nothing to stop these atrocities then or now.)

But what about other victims of such abuse and crimes? My father was lucky compared to most IRS victims. Who will protect them? Congress, the president, the director of the IRS, the county attorney, the sheriff, the local police?

USA Today reported in its July 10, 2013 issue that AIG and GE Capital will face more scrutiny and regulations from the federal government. That's nice isn't it? More scrutiny from government that cannot control its own spending, has our country in catastrophic debt, and continues foreign aid to dozens of countries whose politics are universally corrupt, and whose "moral" policies have us cutting thousands of salaries of low level Department of Defense commissary workers by 20%! Where are the salary cuts of Harry Reid, Nancy Pelosi, Orrin Hatch, or other millionaire politicians? The so-called sequestration cuts by the president involved essential services from low level federal employees, but never once mentioned congressional salaries or cabinet appointees or other high level department heads. (It did go reported that Senator Rand Paul cut his office expenses by 20% and that Mr. Obama cut his own salary by 5%. That must have really hurt considering his salary is $400,000 annually and he and his wife were already millionaires before taking office.) Five per cent, the amazing cut of five per cent!

It cannot be overstated that the IRS has been dishonest in its own accounting, providing no receipts on multi-million dollar "retreats" and "conventions." During its most recent scandal of malfeasance, misappropriation and illegal targeting of constitutional groups, the IRS allotted $50 million for employee bonuses! Twice! Furthermore, FOX News reported that 1100 IRS employees were caught falsifying their own tax records and cheating on their taxes. Were these government workers fired, disciplined, or prosecuted as many Americans have been? No, they were given $1.1 million in bonuses. (Not a smidgen of corruption!) FOX also reported that an EPA employee caught watching porn all day got the same thing: a bonus!

Let's not forget Lois Lerner, the embattled IRS Director, who, when summoned before Congress to explain the illegal and unethical behavior of the IRS, announced that she had done nothing wrong, had nothing to hide, and then arrogantly refused to answer any questions hiding behind her "Fifth Amendment privileges." Should not every citizen be able to do likewise when summoned before IRS Agents? Just tell them you have done nothing wrong, that you have nothing to hide, and then plead the Fifth and go home.

Then, FOX News covered a breaking story on June 13 & 14, 2014, reporting that it took the IRS over one year to provide Congress with the emails and other documents as required by law and that thousands of other emails had been lost in a "hard drive crash." Was that hard drive turned over to Congress for inspection? Not on their life! The "dog ate the homework" and the evidence is gone!

There is only one answer left to summarize this whole dog and pony show: The government is hiding it's own criminal actions. Do you, sheriffs, or do you not have a duty to protect your constituents from such crimes?

Commit the crimes, bungle everything, and get the huge bonuses! Some Republicans are calling for a 25% cut in IRS funding. However, Senator Ted Cruz of Texas is leading a campaign to abolish the IRS! Finally, someone in DC doing something that really matters, that could actually make a difference in the lives of common ordinary American victims, and provide legitimate protection for us all from tyranny! How many of our leaders have joined Senator Cruz in this noble crusade? Remember, the only reason the IRS exists or needs to exist in any shape, manner, or form, is because these same "leaders" who have NOT joined the movement to abolish the IRS, have guaranteed its perpetuity by keeping the tax system unfair, convoluted, and complex!

So, what do our local heads of law enforcement do in response to Federal criminality? Well, make excuses, hide, and of course, continue to pursue more Federal grants! "Well, the feds are going to dish it out somewhere, we might as well get it instead of it going to someone else." Great little system, isn't it? The feds have their own Gestapo collection agency come into the states and counties, forcibly take our money and funnel it to DC bureaucracies! Then, local chiefs and sheriffs grovel before the feds to get some of this stolen money to supplement their own underfunded budgets. **It's not theirs to give and it's not yours to take!**

We the people want to ask every citizen, every chief of police, and each sheriff right now; which system do you favor? The one we just described based on the criminal money game of DC bureaucrats or one in which your local police and sheriff agencies stay independent and predisposed to serve and defend local citizens from tyranny and government abuse? Which one do you want? Undoubtedly, your answer will change if you are audited!

Chapter 9
High Crimes

Yes, we all know politicians lie. We had a chapter about lies previously, but let's take a look at some of the things the U.S. Government has done which are against the law, criminal, or just down right corrupt:

- Creating money out of thin air. Yes, allowing government to just keep printing money regardless of whether or not it is backed by true value (gold or silver) is corrupt and illegal. Yes, we all know it's been going on for a very long time, but its lengthy duration does not make it right or lawful.
- The raiding of the gold that was supposed to be secured in Fort Knox.

- Raiding the Social Security account.
- **Inside trading!** Yes, our politicians in DC take information relating to private businesses being awarded government contracts and then invest in such businesses before the contracts are announced publicly and make a small fortune on the NYSE. Congressman Lamar Smith of Texas has done this numerous times. Each time he did so, he assured voters that it was just a coincidence! (This is the same thing Martha Stewart went to prison for.)
- Taking an oath to uphold and defend the United States Constitution and then summarily ignoring it or even intentionally doing the opposite. This is at the least perjury and at the most treason. It's extremely serious either way. The most glaring example of this is our own U.S. Supreme Court justice Ruth Bader Ginsburg, who publicly announced her personal disdain for the U.S. Constitution and gave her opinion we should all be following a much better constitution, that of South Africa!
- Taking money by force from citizens and then in turn giving it to people the politicians believe are more deserving of it, or even worse, doing this for huge corporations such as AIG, whose bosses received huge bonuses from tax payer dollars.
- Creating a welfare state. (The Founders specifically warned us against such.)
- The Patriot Act.
- The National Defense Authorization Act.
- Forcibly taking money from taxpayers and funneling it to Planned Parenthood and other abortion providers.
- Spending money they do not have and that we cannot afford.

- Bankrupting our nation.
- Distributing Federal grants (the Federal bribery system).
- Paying themselves exorbitant salaries and pensions.
- Enacting "laws" they have never read!
- Assuming regulatory authority where it is not allowed in the Constitution.
- Allowing bureaucracies to destroy rights which are clearly guaranteed in the Bill of Rights.
- Using our military for frivolous and unconstitutional reasons.
- Department of Education using a SWAT team to collect unpaid student loans.
- Involving us in a "War on Terror" and risking the lives of thousands of our young men and women to apprehend the worst terrorists in the world, and then releasing these same terrorists in lopsided prisoner exchange deals.
- Keeping veterans of war on fabricated waiting lists for medical care until they die.
- Federal immigration agents dropping off thousands of illegal aliens, including children, at bus stations in Phoenix and Tucson!
- Running illegal guns to Mexico, claiming no responsibility for it, and then claiming "executive privilege" to stop the entire investigation.
- Using the IRS and FBI to intimidate the President's political opposition.
- Intentionally refusing to secure our borders (Now, hot off the wire, U. S. immigration officials have announced that the Mexican drug cartels have used the chaos at the border to their advantage!)

- Paying Mexico $622 million each year in "foreign aid" and yet doing nothing to secure the release of an innocent marine, Sgt. Andrew Tahmooressi from one of their cockroach prisons. (Maybe we should offer them a prisoner exchange deal... say a few million or so?)

This list could go on and on. It obviously is heading in the wrong direction. Local officials play footsie with DC corrupt politicians in order to keep their share of federal grants. If you bow to this system and take the money, what does that make you? Could it be that you have become part of the problem? You complain about Obama, but then take his grants and bribes! Why?

Not Yours to Give

To underscore the corrupt spending practices of our U S Congress, let's take a look at a powerful lesson by one of our nation's most famous congressmen and frontiersmen, Davy Crockett. Many people don't know or remember that Crockett actually served four years in the U.S. Congress. Crockett's historic political position was overshadowed by his famous last stand at the Alamo in Texas in 1836, in which he gave his life while standing with Texans for liberty.

At one point in his political career, Crockett was out campaigning for re-election and stopped by a farm in his district. The farmer welcomed Davy to his property, but assured him that he would be not voting for him again. The farmer told Davy that he did not believe him to be dishonest, but that his understanding and interpretation of the Constitution were very different than his. "The man who wields power and misinterprets it, is more dangerous the more honest he is," the farmer explained. The congressman was bewildered and assured the man that he could not recall voting on any constitutional issue in the recent past.

The farmer patiently explained that Davy had voted to authorize a $20,000 payment from the general fund to some families suffering from the effects of a horrible fire in Georgetown. Crockett admitted to doing so and even excused such with, "surely a country as rich as ours can afford to help in relieving the suffering of women and children."

The farmer let Crockett have his say, but chastised him afterward for his faulty opinion. "The power of collecting and dispersing money at pleasure is the most dangerous power that can be entrusted to man. You may attempt to relieve a burden on one person, but increase them on many others, who may very well be worse off than the person you are helping. The amount is not important, you had as much a right to give $20 million as you did the $20,000. The Constitution does not define charity or authorize charitable contributions. Congress has no right to give charity!"

The farmer explained that members of congress could have given their own money to such charities, but instead chose to give money belonging to the taxpayers. "The money you gave was not yours to give," he said.

Crockett was ashamed and could not argue with his constituent. In fact, Congressman Crockett told the farmer that he had heard many speeches in Congress, but that the man's speech from his plow was the best he had ever heard.

Congress, by law, holds the purse strings for our nation. But when they dish money out in unauthorized ways (as they so routinely do) that money is not theirs to give! And it is not *yours* to take!

These federal crimes, especially those of the IRS, will continue until sheriffs and local authorities do something to stop it! It will not stop because you tell IRS victims to get a lawyer or to vote the crooks out!

Government is not the solution to the problem, government *is* the problem! Congressional attempts to solve the problems of one group by taking money from another is not a proper use of public funds and doing so *is not charity*!

Chapter 10
With Thunderous Applause

In Star Wars Episode III, Revenge Of The Sith, a particular scene involved Senator Padmé Amidala, played by Natalie Portman, who fought to preserve peace and freedom throughout the galaxy. When the Senate voted to give additional powers to the chancellor (i.e. more power to the central government and less to the local governments), to combat a supposed threat, the majority responded with huge applause at its successful passing. Lamenting the passage of the evil and destructive statute, Senator Amidala said, "So this is how liberty dies... with thunderous applause."

One only has to watch the Democratic or Republican national conventions or partisan state conventions to witness the reality of America dying "with thunderous applause." So many cheer as we elect time and time again career politicians who lie and cheat and lust for power. They promise to follow the Constitution and do precisely the opposite. They steal money and then decide who needs the stolen funds and summarily pass it out "to the less fortunate" and parade around like heroes, showing how magnanimous they can be with others people's money! They create disasters such as Agenda 21, Common Core, NDAA, Obamacare, etc.

In fact, what the feds have not thoroughly destroyed of our nation's food supply, they have turned over to Monsanto, who now has a monopoly on genetically modifying the remainder of the supply. In fact, they have genetically altered 99% of all corn grown in the USA. This process has created such a "Frankenstein" with all its mass manipulation of our food that now our nation's honey bees are dying!

Every American should wonder why our own government is destroying our food supply, buying up billions of rounds of ammunition, and now, destroying our health care system.

Such self-granting power as "Obamacare" is clearly not allowed within the Constitution's parameters, yet we got it anyway, and "with thunderous applause." Obama forces us as "free" Americans to take his version of what's best for our own personal health. Socialism and liberty cannot co-exist and never have. The one constant with "socialistic reforms" is that they are always cleverly sold to the public as benevolent programs to help the poor and make us "equal." The truth is that such government "help" is more control, more subjugation, and a means to make government bigger and more expensive. But, as long as it's for our own good and as long as it gives Chris Matthews a "tingle up his leg," then we should be okay.

Of course, the Gestapo of America, the IRS, is hiring thousands more agents and has been selected by Mr. Obama to enforce his "taking care of us" health care plan! The most ruthless and scandal-ridden agency ever to exist on American soil, and **they** have been chosen to make sure we comply with Obama's "caring and kind" attempt to provide us all with health care! Absolute insanity!

For you excuse makers; why don't you be upfront with your pro-government, pro-corruption views? Campaign honestly and let your voters know that you will not stand for liberty, that you will allow the feds to come into your county and do whatever they like! Let your constituents know that you will not stop government abuse or crimes and that you will exercise no authority to prevent them from being victimized by government criminals. Let your citizens know that you will not serve them or protect their lands and businesses from government criminals!

When all government shall be drawn to Washington as the center of all power, it will render powerless the checks [constitution] and become as venal and oppressive as the government from which we separated.

~ Thomas Jefferson

You potential Davids out there, with sling in hand: Do you say that only Goliath can stop Goliath?

Richard Mack | *Are You A David?*

Chapter 11
The Last Five Years

The last five years have been the epitome of roller coaster rides. There have been highs and lows, fulfillment and disappointment, and enough twists and turns to make anyone sick! Let's take a brief look back.

The awakening in America really took off as a result of the 2008 election. Many of us were thrilled that some newcomer to the national stage was beating Hillary Clinton! Then when Obama did beat her we ended up with something worse: both Hillary **and** Obama. The Republican candidate was not much better and Glenn Beck even opined that John McCain would have been worse than Obama had he won the presidency. As difficult as that might be to imagine, yes, McCain has supported Obama many times and is quite the socialist himself. All three of these mainstream 2008 candidates for President support the tax, borrow, and spend corruption of Washington DC politics and have done nothing to rein in out-of-control bureaucracies or promote fundamental freedom for American citizens.

This set of conditions gave birth to the predecessor to this book, *The County Sheriff: America's Last Hope.* My belief that there was still a peaceful way to take back our country and literally make Washington DC irrelevant was my primary motivation for writing that book, and it continues in this sequel. There is hope!

In pursuance of peaceful solutions, this book and the roller coaster ride took off! As soon as the book was published, calls and requests for the book and for speaking engagements went through the roof! Tea party groups called and asked me to attend their rallies. I made appearances at over over 120 Tea Party events ranging from Maui to Bangor, Maine. We could not keep the book on the shelf. Internet orders were nearly impossible to keep up with. I had not anticipated any of this and did not have the infrastructure in place to deal with it all. This was some of the high part of the "ride." It was so exciting to see all the commotion about my book, but there were some lows right along with it. National publications went after me with a vengeance! I got hate mail from police officers and other politicians. I've had some people get so infuriated with me as I explained the dangers of gun control that it made me grateful that they did not believe in guns, because if they had had one in their possession at the time, they undoubtedly would have shot me! That happened at a very liberal event at the University of Colorado where I was invited to be one of five "conservatives" appearing on the panels. There were approximately 105 panelists. Yes, only five out of 105 were American conservatives!

I spoke at a Police Academy graduation in Missouri, was the keynote speaker at the Kentucky Sheriffs' Association banquet, and was a guest lecturer at over a dozen universities all across America, including ten such lectures in BYU's political science classes. I was just recently invited to appear at the New York state capital in Albany to a speak at a press conference held by other legislators there, who wanted my input about the unconstitutionality of the New York SAFE act. I have been to every state (I just went to Alaska in May of this year to advise them regarding an effort to create their own sheriff's offices there, something which they have not had before) and have hundreds of thousands of frequent flier miles with the major airlines, and some not so major.

On the other hand, I was invited to speak at the Mississippi State Sheriffs' conference three years ago and then got canceled because their President found out that I was "too controversial." The other NSA (National Sheriffs' Association), has an annual convention where hundreds of vendors purchase booths to display their wares that might appeal to our country's sheriffs and law officers. I submitted an application for just a one table booth and put my form of payment on the application. You guessed it. I was declined because they heard I was "too controversial." If there is anything I have learned over the past 20 years, (that's been especially reinforced over the past five) it is that the only thing you have to do to be "controversial" is to quote the Constitution or the Founding Fathers, or disagree with mainstream political correctness! And heaven forbid, never go against the money laundering and bribery system as presently constituted between the feds and our nation's law enforcement agencies! And don't object to all the police raids and SWAT teams and asset forfeitures that our nation's "finest" administer, where they keep the monies and goods collected during such raids to augment their own budgets! If you go along with such "programs" you'll definitely be invited to attend and even speak at NSA conventions. But **NEVER** bring up the need for adherence to our oaths of office or actually defending individual liberty! That's way too controversial!

America Is Dying!

Yes, the last five years have seen a dramatic and sickening shift in our attitudes towards the law. It used to be that politicians at least tried to hide their dirty deeds. Now, offenses against the Constitution – the supreme law of the land – are carried out routinely and blatantly, without the least fear of any reprimand. We're so jaded we don't even expect a rationalization anymore! It starts with our nation's head and trickles all the way down.

What are you, the Sheriff, guardian of the peace and the ultimate protector of the people, going to do about it? Perhaps you will do nothing, because it's just not your responsibility. Or, you will keep doing what we have always done. Why? Because that's the way we have always done things! Many simply ignore the issue altogether and go back to work applying for more federal grants. Obtaining "free money" is one of the best ways to serve the citizens we work for. That way we get our fair share of what's rightfully ours!

We will go along because our county needs a new bridge or a new jail, so we grovel before the King to get his allowance. Arizona Governor Jan Brewer assailed Obamacare until he offered her two billion dollars to "expand medicare." Then she held a public rally to announce her acquiescence "with thunderous applause." We do the same for a new NSA complex or a new Homeland Security office, or a new housing project or a new dam. We're sure it will help our citizens if we have these projects thriving in our community. It's called community-ism! Oh, whoops, the spell check failed; it's actually called communism.

Franklin D Roosevelt called it the "New Deal," Lyndon Johnson called it the "War on Poverty," Bush called it "compassionate conservatism,"and Obama calls it "Affordable Healthcare." No matter what the propaganda ploys were or are, the final analysis is clear: these programs are all socialism or communism.

When the government controls the land, the jobs, the air, all waterways, industries, pensions, health care, education, and the re-distribution of wealth, the conclusion is inescapable; **it's communism!** Many of these practices come directly from the United Nations and its implementation of Agenda 21.

Richard Mack | *Are You A David?*

Chapter 12
Badge vs. Badge

In the 2003 Winter issue of *Range* magazine, a powerful article appeared about three western sheriffs who were fighting yet another federal battle with the Bureau of Land Management (BLM). The sheriffs were trying to "serve and protect" some of their ranchers and farmers who were being harassed to the point of losing their businesses due to the overreach of the BLM. You see, the federal government runs the land and regulates how cows and horses can "eat grass" otherwise known as "grazing rights" which are all bestowed upon ranchers by the omnipotent federal government. So the sheriffs interposed on behalf of their citizens. This is the doctrine of interposition that James Madison spoke of in his famous Virginia Resolution.

...whenever the federal government exceeds its constitutional limits and begins to oppress the citizens of a state, that state's legislature is duty bound to *interpose* its power to prevent the federal government from victimizing its people.

~ James Madison

The state's legislature is not the only state entity "duty bound" to *interpose* its power to protect the people from the feds! Everyone elected or appointed within any of the state's political subdivisions has the same responsibility.

But, if ranchers don't do the grazing correctly or if they allow their cattle to step on a desert tortoise or some other "endangered species," then the feds will descend upon your property and confiscate your herds so the land and turtles can be protected! Who protects the ranchers and their businesses, their pursuit of happiness, and their families? That is a very good question! One that will be answered by three sheriffs, Jones, Penrod, and Aman. "In many a shire, the reeve has just about had it with the feds."

"What they really want is to extend federal authority over all law enforcement in the United States, whether local people agree with it or not," says Jones. "Well, it's 'not' in this county." The BLM supervisor even asked Sheriff Jones if he would deputize them all so that the BLM agents could write tickets to Eureka County residents and *all the money would go to Eureka County!* "I told him to have his agents find the nearest pay phone and call 9-1-1, and I'd give them the same authority as everyone else in the county," said Sheriff Jones.

"Local people have come to me again and again about horse gathers or cattle seizures or property rights and asked me to defend them from their own government. I don't blame them, sometimes the government scares me, too."

Standing even when you are scared is the true definition of courage!

Just north of Nevada in Owyhee County, Idaho, Sheriff Gary Aman developed a unique agreement with the BLM which limited where they could go within the county. All of this occurred pursuant to complaints Sheriff Aman received from his ranchers and farmers. Sheriff Aman made it very clear to the BLM that he would not only arrest environmental activists, but federal agents as well if they did not comply with the "agreement." (Aman's policy) "I just said that I expect them to obey the law in my county the same way they expect ranchers to obey regulations on federal land." The Owyhee County Commissioners sided with the Sheriff and put forth a united effort in defending Owyhee County ranchers. The end result was freedom, peace, and the enforcement of property rights! Such an occurrence does not happen by chance or by sitting back and wishing the feds would be more user friendly!

Sheriff Gary Penrod from San Bernardino County, California, (one of the nation's biggest and most complex counties) has had similar problems with the BLM. Sheriff Penrod revoked local law enforcement authority from the federal government and advised them to consult with him before taking any action on private property. Penrod said that part of his decision came from just being fed up with the confusion caused by federal agents challenging local residents who had lived there for generations. "Both sides seem to get along much better now that the line is drawn," said Penrod. "I think that we've been able to send out the message that we're not going to be run over by Big Brother."

How could these three sheriffs do such things? Where did they get the authorization to take such stands? In fact, even one had his county commissioners standing with him! Doesn't the federal government trump the local authorities in all matters? Shouldn't these sheriffs have gone to court and asked permission to keep their oaths from federal judges?

Did you notice the equation?

**Constitutional county commissioners
plus Constitutional sheriffs
equals
LIBERTY!**

Sheriffs standing for liberty and protecting their citizens "from all enemies, both foreign and domestic," is nothing new! Sometimes though, such worthy stories just don't make headlines or receive their due from NBC, CBS, or ABC. Sometimes they don't receive their due from any media whatsoever or from other sheriffs! RANGE magazine, and of course, the CSPOA, (Constitutional Sheriffs And Peace Officers Association) and the author of *They Fired The First Shot* expose these hero sheriffs for the great work they have done. Ask the ranchers and farmers in Owyhee County, Idaho, San Bernardino County, California, (Yes, even in California!) and Eureka County, Nevada if they believe in the power of the Sheriff and if he indeed is THE LAST LINE IN THE SAND, America's last real hope!

Chapter 13
Josie The Outlaw

Josie Wales, better known on the Internet as Josie the Outlaw, is an average American, a waitress and bartender from Philadelphia. She's produced some amazing videos that have been all over the web, where she has asked some simple and poignant questions to our nation's police. She wants to know if there is anything that legislatures can pass that our nation's peace officers would refuse to go along with. Many Americans are looking for similar answers, many of whom, are discovering the same eternal truth, that tyrants never cease their own tyranny. Josie articulates her questions better than anyone else. The following are her own words:

If you work in law enforcement, I have a very

important question for you, one which soon may be a matter of life or death. I'm sure some people become police officers just so they can boss other people around. But I'm going to assume that you mean well, and that you want to be one of the good guys, in which case, my question is this: Is there anything the politicians could enact into law that you would not enforce? Is there any order that you would refuse to carry out? Or will you do absolutely anything your bosses tell you to?

In the U.S., police have already obeyed orders to fine or arrest people for a wide variety of harmless activities, such as dancing at the Jefferson Memorial, or having a vegetable garden in their front yard. Police have even gone so far as to execute violent paramilitary raids on food co-ops and organic farms.

For decades, police have been carrying out armed home invasions, forced property confiscations, and other acts of violence against people who weren't hurting anyone, but who engaged in behaviors or habits which law-makers have arbitrarily declared to be illegal.

You may be comfortable in assuming that you'll never receive an order to do something truly immoral, but the fact is, with every order you receive, you have a choice, between obeying without question, or relying on your conscience. No doubt there were cops a few years ago, who never expected to be ordered to disarm innocent people, to do door-to-door home searches without warrant or probable cause, or to detain and interrogate people for merely driving down a road. Yet police have since been ordered to do all of these things, and almost without exception, they obeyed. So it's not unreasonable to ask, is there any point at which you will draw a line and say, "No, that I will not do"?

And if you won't draw such a line anywhere--if you will do absolutely anything your political masters tell you to--how are you any different from the enforcers of Soviet Russia, Red China, or Nazi Germany? You may be tempted to say, "I don't make the law, I just enforce it," or to argue that if some legislature, court, or some authority above you says its okay, then it must be. But keep in mind, that this is exactly what the thugs of every tyrannical regime in history said to justify their actions. And how do we remember those people now? As courageous, noble law enforcers? No. Unless you want posterity remembering YOU as a heartless, mindless pawn of oppression, then you'd better decide--and decide now--where you will draw that line.

Unfortunately, there is little indication that most cops have any line at all. The incidents of police officers refusing to inflict injustice upon the people are extremely rare. Even when cops say they personally oppose certain laws, such as marijuana prohibition, nearly all of them continue to violently enforce those laws against nonviolent people. In other words, they recognize some laws as counterproductive and unjust, but they choose to enforce them anyway.

For the most part, American cops seem completely incapable of disobeying immoral orders, and instead do what the enforcers of every other authoritarian empire have done, inflicting harm on innocent people whenever and however those in power tell them to, while accepting no personal responsibility for their actions. I hope you are better than that.

Keep in mind, there are a lot of decent Americans who do have the integrity and courage to draw a line in the sand, a point at which they will disobey and resist violations of their rights by those in power. It may be that they refuse to be disarmed. It may be that they refuse to cooperate with warrantless searches, or refuse to keep funding a government they view as destructive and unjust. Whether you agree with them doesn't particularly matter. What does matter is whether, in the end, you are willing, if and when you are ordered to do so, to violently assault the dissenters for their disobedience.

When they draw their line in the sand, and stand their ground, and your supervisors tell you to use whatever level of violence necessary to get submission and compliance from the resisters, will you obey? If it came down to it, would you kill American citizens for disobeying politicians?

Now, if someone is actually harming someone else, of course you have the right to use whatever force necessary to stop the attacker and protect the innocent, but that would be the case even if you had no badge and no uniform. But when you try to arrest someone who hasn't threatened or harmed anyone else, but has only disobeyed some arbitrary regulation, then you are the one initiating force, you are the one starting a fight, you are the bad guy.

Now remember, the American Revolution was people forcibly resisting gun confiscation, warrantless searches, what they viewed as unfair taxation, and a number of other oppressions, all in the name of "law," all carried out by "law enforcers." If you had lived back then, would you have been among the rebel colonists, the ones who refused to be disarmed, refused to pay taxes, and resisted warrantless detainment and searches? Would you have sided with the signers of the Declaration of Independence, or would you have been among the redcoats, the "law enforcers," assaulting, caging or killing any colonist with the gall to disobey the king? And which side are you on today?

Of course, the message you'll get from your superiors, the politicians, and your fellow officers, is that it's not your place to decide which laws to enforce, and that as long as you faithfully follow orders, that you can't be held personally responsible for doing as you're told. But that is a lie. A horribly dangerous lie.

At the Nuremberg trials, it was established that the excuse used by the Nazi law enforcers, that they weren't to blame and shouldn't be punished because they were just doing as they were told, did not relieve them of personal responsibility for their actions. And make no mistake: if you choose to blindly obey unjust commands, and one day your intended victims decide to fight back, saying that you're "just doing your job" will not make you bullet-proof. It may be your own life you save by deciding now at what point you will choose to be a moral, responsible human being, instead of just an obedient pawn of those in power.

Ultimately, only you can answer the question of where you will draw that line, but really, the only moral, rational answer is this: if something would be wrong for you to do without a badge, then you shouldn't do it with one either. The idea that uniforms and legislation can give you special rights, is both false and horribly dangerous. Nearly every large-scale injustice in history was committed by people who wrongly imagined that their position of authority made it okay for them to do things that other people have no right to do.

Like everyone else, you have the right to use force to stop attackers and protect the innocent, and when you do that, you are the hero. But you have no right to be the attacker, even if it's your job, and even if the aggression is called "law." Always, in every situation, you and you alone are responsible

for what you do. Wearing a badge and a uniform, and doing whatever you're told, does not make you brave and noble, or deserving of any respect. "Just following orders" is a coward's excuse. If your job requires you to assault or cage people who haven't threatened or harmed anyone, then quit.

Being an actual protector--doing the RIGHT thing, no matter what anyone else says, even if it means disobeying orders and breaking the law—that takes courage and integrity. That makes you a hero. So, do you have enough of a spine to draw that line? Decide now, before your failure to think for yourself results in damage that cannot be undone.

So very well said, and such a profound and penetrating question from an average American with a desire to be free. Josie, knowing full well that freedom is defined by the extent to which government leaves us alone, asks our police if they will. Or, if they will continue to treat Americans as subjects, suspects, and peasants and excuse such with "I don't make the laws." There can never be any moral justification for doing that which is absolutely immoral. Even if such immorality is in the form of legislation laced with good intentions! The bottom line is; Josie has asked a very sincere and reasonable question and she is more than deserving of an answer. So, what is your answer? She has a right to know!

The methodology and tactics utilized are *your* choice, patrol officer. Even if you were trained to beat someone as the cops claimed in the Rodney King incident, that does not mean you have to do it! Just because SCOTUS declares "road blocks" and DUI checkpoints to be constitutional, that does not mean you have to do them!

Josie is right; the police stop Americans for merely driving down the road. What is the probable cause for such stops? "The Supreme Court said we could" is *not* probable cause! *It's an excuse!*

We could all learn a lot from Josie. Then again, we could also learn a lot from Sam, George, John, James, Patrick, and Thomas.

The essence of tyranny is the enforcement of stupid laws.

- Edmund Burke

Chapter 14
What If We Had Hundreds Like Them?

The sheriffs mentioned in this book are not the only constitutional sheriffs in America. Sheriff Dave Mattis from Wyoming set the example in the 90's and many others have been very dedicated to their oaths and to their constituents. Clearly these constitutional sheriffs have dispelled the excuses made so infamous by the sheriffs and officials who choose not to stand for liberty. What would America be like today if we had hundreds of sheriffs emulating some of the people below?

Sheriff David A. Clarke, Milwaukee County, Wisconsin

Sheriff Clarke stood for the Second Amendment in such a novel and creative way, releasing public service announcements through the local media asking his citizens to arm themselves, to be trained and ready to help him fight crime! The county commissioners and the Milwaukee chief of police fought Sheriff Clarke all the way. Sheriff Clarke stood all the stronger! Sheriff Clarke is 6'5" weighs about 225, wears a cowboy hat and shiny boots, and carries with him a pocket Constitution everywhere he goes. When Sheriff Clarke talks; people listen. His speech at the CSPOA summer convention of 2013 in Missouri had the crowd spellbound. We highly recommend it to each of you.

Sheriff Clarke was the CSPOA 2013 Sheriff of the Year and accepted the award during a power outage at the Ameristar Hotel in St. Charles, Missouri, due to a nearby tornado.

Sheriff Glenn Palmer, Grant County, Oregon

Sheriff Palmer has taken his oath of allegiance to the Constitution very seriously and campaigns every four years on that principle. He has been fighting to protect his citizens from the overreach of the U.S. Forest Service for well over a decade, *interposing* himself on behalf of his constituents. Sheriff Palmer asked a very profound question also; he asked the USFS where they received their authority and what provision of the Constitution explains such authority. He has never received an answer.

Police Chief James Craig, Detroit, Michigan

Chief James has been known for encouraging gun ownership for the citizens in his jurisdiction. Here is an article regarding the effect this has had on crime in his city.

The chief of Detroit police credited legally armed residents for a substantial decrease in crime in a city that desperately needs it.

"Criminals are getting the message that good Detroiters are armed and will use that weapon," said chief James Craig, according to The Detroit News.

"I don't want to take away from the good work our investigators are doing, but I think part of the drop in crime, and robberies in particular, is because criminals are thinking twice that citizens could be armed."

According to The Detroit News, there have been 37 percent fewer robberies, 22 percent fewer break-ins and 30 percent fewer carjackings this so far in 2014 compared to the same period last year.

"I can't say what specific percentage is caused by this, but there's no question in my mind it has had an effect," Craig said.

The chief cited fewer stories of Detroit homeowners having to fire weapons at intruders as evidence that criminals are getting the message.

The Motor City has been the poster-child of urban crisis for several decades. For various reasons the city has fallen deeply into debt, leading to what has been dubbed a "death spiral" of cutbacks to public services and increasing crime.

Craig's pro-self-defense comments are not new. He was featured in a National Rifle Association publication earlier this year and has made other statements to the press claiming that an armed citizenry helps deter crime.

In his remarks, Craig distinguished between the effects of gun ownership among law-abiding citizens and ownership among criminals.

"[Criminals] automatically assume another criminal is carrying," Craig said. "I'm talking about criminals who are thinking of robbing a citizen; they're less likely to do so if they think they might be armed."

Al Woods, an ex-criminal in the city, backed Craig's claims.

"If I was out there now robbing people these days, knowing there are a lot more people with guns, I know I'd have to rethink my game plan," Woods told The Detroit News.

~ The Daily Caller, The Detroit News

Sheriff Jeff Christopher, Sussex County, Delaware

Sheriff Christopher wants to be a constitutional sheriff. He is dedicated to the principles of liberty and American ideals. He wants to *enforce* the law and the Constitution, but he can't! His county commissioners say he cannot enforce the law, or manage his own office, conduct the hiring and firing of his own employees, or make any arrests. No, they are not his bosses or supervisors, but they do it anyway and the courts have said it's legal. Sheriff Christopher fought it. He lost. (That's Delaware!) The State Attorney General, Beau Biden (no the fruit does not fall far from the tree) gave his legal opinion, that the sheriffs in Delaware do not have the power or authority to make arrests! Even though the State Constitution clearly states that the sheriff is "the conservator of the peace." Biden and the courts have failed to explain how the sheriff is the conservator of the peace yet has no capability to arrest those who violate the peace! Thus, the further destruction to the office of sheriff along the Eastern sea board. Sheriff Christopher has valiantly waged this battle to save the office of sheriff. It has not gone well at all.

Sheriffs in Connecticut should have done the same when the State voted the office of sheriff into near extinction about 14 years ago, turning all law enforcement over to the police state. The state police are bureaucrats and answer to other bureaucrats, not to the people. The sheriffs in Connecticut all went along with this destruction of our Republic and took the high-paying state marshal jobs they were offered. The only sheriff to fight this move was Sheriff Joe Arpaio from Arizona. He went and testified before the Connecticut legislature as to how they were making the mistake of their lives. They did not listen. Having ears, they heard not!

What if we had more sheriffs and police chiefs like these? Certainly they are not the only ones standing, interposing, and protecting their constituents, and there are more mentioned in other chapters.

The potential for freedom is here. It's in your hands. The solution is in your county. Support your local David; he works for you!

Chapter 15
TIME Magazine: Does The Constitution Matter?

In the July 4, 2011, issue of *TIME* magazine, Managing Editor Richard Stengel, calls the Constitution "elastic" and even goes so far as to claim that was exactly what the Founders intended to do; make the Constitution flexible and mutable. To follow this "logic" and revisionist philosophy, *TIME* would have us all believe that the Framers of our Constitution were merely forming a new government based on generalities and ideas of moral and situational relativity, certain of only one thing, that future generations would hammer out something that might preserve some semblance of the "democracy" the Founding Fathers were leaving us. (It was actually a Republic. The word 'Democracy' is never mentioned in the Constitution, but how would we expect *TIME*'s Managing Editor to know that?) *TIME* stays deeply within its own mainstream culture to convince us all that everything going on in government today is exactly as it was intended. The Constitution has no absolutes, it was not written as a limitation, for so *TIME* declared. (And of course *TIME* and Stengel do this to celebrate our nation's *Independence Day*!)

In fact, Stengel makes two very startling, if not downright bewildering claims. First, and quoting, "Politicians ask all the time, What would the Framers say?" Wow! Really? Today's politicians ask all the time, "What would the Framers say?" Please show me one time! I have never heard Barak Obama say such a thing. When was the last time Nancy Pelosi asked, "What would the Framers say?" How about John McCain, Harry Reid, Mitt Romney, John Kerry, Mayor Bloomberg, Chris Christie, any of these politicians who are in the news daily; when did any of them ask about the Framers' intentions? Secondly, and even more astonishing, the managing editor of a major international publication informs us all that we can never know what the Framers said or what they meant: "They're gone, they are all dead. They are no longer part of the American political debate."

So, according to *TIME* magazine, we cannot look at the intent of the Founding Fathers nor learn from their wisdom because "...they're not around to prove anyone wrong." I guess we should all ignore the Federalist Papers, and all the other journals and writings of the Framers. We should ignore the warnings of Patrick Henry in his fiery "Give me Liberty or Give me Death" speech, or Thomas Paine's Common Sense booklet or the biography of John Adams which quotes many of his beliefs in letters he wrote to his wife, Abigail. Perhaps when we all walk through the Jefferson Memorial, we should ignore the quotes on the walls about freedom and Jefferson's passion for American idealism. We can't know what the Framers intended when they wrote the Bill of Rights or what on earth they could have meant when they proclaimed, "Congress shall make no law..." How convenient for our "leaders" that they "interpret" such ambiguity for us all! What would we do without them? Could the Founders have actually intended that these rules and supreme laws should be **obeyed** instead of "interpreted?" Was the Bill of Rights written to protect inviolable principles? Nah! The Bill of Rights did nothing to limit government. Why? Because *TIME* said the Framers knew nothing "about airplanes, computers, miniskirts, or Lady Gaga!" (Yes, that is a direct quote!) In other words, we don't have to follow the Bill of Rights today, because, according to *TIME*, we don't know what the Framers really intended and *TIME* thinks if they did intend anything, it was all elastic and entirely flexible anyway!

Therefore, when the Founders fought for freedom and – subsequent to the Revolutionary War – wrote the Constitution and required within it (Article VI last paragraph) that each soldier, each judge, all legislators, all peace officers, and even the President himself, must swear an oath of allegiance to uphold it, that they meant only as far as they agreed with its elasticity. When the Founders said the Constitution would be the chains by which all leaders would be bound, they meant only sort of bound, with elastic cords, perhaps even less confining than rubber bands, but certainly not *chains*! Thus, accountability by our leaders is negated as there are no absolute rules to hold them to.

So *TIME* claims that the Constitution (including the Bill of Rights) is not absolute, that it contains mere guidelines and suggestions. Yet the government enforces voluminous and ambiguous IRS codes as if they are entirely absolute. And what about the thousands and thousands of traffic statutes? Police pretend that such "laws" are *absolutely* absolute and hide behind bushes to pounce on unsuspecting citizens and plunder their substance at the drop of a hat. In other words, the Bill of Rights and the principles therein *are not absolute, but the traffic laws and criminal codes are!* How can we live under such hypocrisy and survive as a country and neighbors?

Yes, Mr. Stengel, you and *TIME* are demonstrating once again that you have earned the title of "Lamestream Media." You attempt to rationalize away our sacred Constitution and thereby assist with the mainstream destruction of what the *FRAMERS and FOUNDING FATHERS* established in the first place.

The one valid point *TIME* magazine made in this 4th of July celebration issue was portraying a photograph of the United States Constitution in shreds. And nothing is more evident of this shredding than *TIME*'s/Stengel's idiotic explanation as to why politicians no longer follow the Constitution. No, none of us knows what the Framers would have said about Lady Gaga. But most likely they would have been horrified by forced socialistic health care, a $17 trillion national debt, and a bunch of corrupt politicians in DC ignoring the Constitution. Certainly, many politicians thank *TIME* and Stengel for easing their consciences on why we don't follow the supreme laws of the land anymore.

The man who reads nothing at all is better educated than the man who reads nothing but newspapers.

~ **Thomas Jefferson**

I think that with a little elasticity we can apply Jefferson's quote to magazines as well, since the Founders didn't know about them. It's amazing how intelligent and prophetic the Framers really were!

Chapter 16
No Excessive Fines or Bail

It really is not that difficult to examine history to determine the intent of the Founders regarding the ideals they hoped to secure within the structure of the Constitution. The Eighth Amendment is certainly no exception to the rule. One of the abuses the Founders intended to prevent was the out-of-control issuance of fines (citations) and the subsequent bail required in their "Redcoat" courts.

> **Excessive bail shall not be required, nor excessive fines imposed, nor cruel and unusual punishment inflicted.**
>
> **- Eighth Amendment to the U.S. Constitution**

Such excessive "fines or bail" were commonplace. Has it ended? Not hardly! Today we have our police doing the same thing and the courts rubber-stamping this "taxation through citation" process as if no Eighth Amendment ever existed!

There is no fairness, there is no chance for the citizen to win against this enormous system of the contemporary version of "Redcoat" collection tactics. Traffic court throughout America is so one-sided and stacked against the citizen that any hope for justice is as ridiculous a proposition as obtaining a fair hearing with the IRS! Traffic courts, whether conducted by justices of the peace, municipal judges, clerks, hearing officers, or whoever the government appoints to go through the collection motions, is a system designed to do one thing and one thing only: *collect the money!*

In most states, you are not allowed an "impartial jury" or any jury at all, as required by the Sixth Amendment. The Seventh Amendment also grants that *"the right of trial by jury shall be preserved"* in any suit exceeding $20. So, are these supreme laws of the land "preserved" in Boise, Idaho, Gilbert, Arizona, Lehi, Utah (one of the worst court systems in America) or Punta Gorda, Florida? No! Why not? Because such requirements and rules impede the free exercise of C-O-L-L-E-C-T-I-O-N-S! If the states and cities followed the rules then "collections" would be severely diminished. You can't allow that!

Arizona has made traffic citations "civil" infractions. Why? You guessed it! Because civil procedures require less evidence to convict the accused and thus, collection of the fines is easier or more cost effective. The message has gone out loud and clear to all Americans, you have no chance of winning in any traffic court anywhere, so just save the time and trouble and pay your fine; just get it over with. The officer does not have to present any evidence against you, the only thing he has to do is say you did it. Guilty! His word against yours; you will lose every time!

A citizen was recently given a traffic citation for failure to wear a seat belt while traveling a city street in rural Arizona. He chose to challenge the unconstitutional ticket in court, as he had a right to do. At the hearing, the judge (after ruling that the ticket had to be paid) actually reprimanded him for wasting the court's time, saying that the fee on the ticket wasn't even enough to pay for the time of the judge and officer who had to attend (as though it was unpatriotic of him to ask for his constitutionally guaranteed day in court).

Does this system have any rule or preconceived notion that any benefit of the doubt is on the side of the citizen? Is any part of this system based on "innocent until proven guilty?" What? Are you kidding? Is it reasonable? Is it fair and impartial? Does it have anything to do with justice? Yes, it should, but it simply and lamentably, does not even pretend to. Just pay your "fair share" and go home and hope you don't get your car impounded the next time you are stopped. If you fail the "attitude test" that could happen very easily. Besides, you can always be grateful that the fines in your state don't even come close to the ridiculous excessiveness of California fines. For a citation in Arizona or Utah that carries a fine of $250, in California the same citation would bring in about $700, or even more! How else can they balance their corrupt budgets and pay for their exorbitant government salaries and pensions? The peasants pay and "that's the ways it has always been!" Besides, who is to say that any of this is "excessive?"

Only the U.S. Supreme Court can make that determination and until then, well, government will keep right on doing what it has always been doing! **"No excessive fines or bail"** are rules every judge and legislator have sworn to obey and if they don't do it then the police have to go along? Absolutely not! Yes, every peace officer in America could stop this abuse and the fleecing of the American people.

Judges all over the country who swear an oath to obey the Constitution before they can take their jobs, refuse to allow *any* Constitutional objections or issues to be brought up in court by defendants! The judges order defendants to leave the Constitution out of their courtrooms with a whopper of an excuse that their court is not the proper forum to determine if the police action against the accused was constitutional.

So, a local or municipal judge, who is lawfully required to swear to obey the Constitution, does not have to do one thing in his courtroom to actually follow the Constitution or ever allow a defendant inside his courtroom to use the Constitution in his own defense!

If the courts don't have to follow the Constitution and the legislators don't have to follow the Constitution, and the cops only have to follow the judges and lawmakers, then who in America has to follow the Constitution? Perhaps that just leaves the U.S. Supreme Court? No they don't have to either, they only have to *interpret* the Constitution! They can, therefore, mold it as they choose. Even if the Supreme Court issues rulings substantiating the Constitution, who then is obligated to enforce the Court's decision? The President of the United States is supposed to. Is there any punishment affixed if he does not do it? No! Then who can the people turn to for help and protection?

When government becomes venal and oppressive, to whom can the people turn for peace, safety, and liberty? Not only do some refuse to answer the call to serve and protect, they actually refuse to answer any question as to how they intend to keep their oath and preserve the Constitution!

The law enforcement community has a habit of pointing fingers at the judges and legislators to blame them for the injustice of the justice system. We are not puppets for the legislative or judicial branches. We have sworn an oath to obey the Constitution just as they have. Why would we allow ourselves to be part of such an obvious violation of the Bill of Rights? We do not have to do this! We certainly can do more to stop it! We are not tax collectors, but the people fear us just the same. We can earn back the public trust by being reasonable, fair, friendly and honorable. We can be Oath Keepers and *Davids!*

The solution is all too simple. Its implementation is perhaps more difficult if not complicated. However, both the simplicity of the solution and complexity of its execution boil down to one simple truth: the courage to act. The solution for the Israelites was simple in concept; David only had to send a single stone from his sling into Goliath's forehead. The implementation, however, took amazing faith and courage. It is the same for us. The door to liberty is wide open. Now we need the courage and faith to walk through it.

In USA Today 6-20-14 issue, Paulina Firozi reported that several local and municipal governments (including the State of Illinois and New Jersey) have passed laws banning police agencies from requiring quotas in their departments' issuance of traffic tickets and that such quotas cannot be used for evaluating police performance.

> **We want to get away from municipalities and officials who look at their police as golden geese and motorists, not as individuals, but as marks whose pockets can be picked.**
>
> **~ Declan O'Scanlon, assemblyman**

New Jersey wants its citizens to believe that their police officers are trying to help people instead of just meeting quotas, and we applaud them for their efforts! Still, it emphasizes how bad the problem has become. Ticket writing has been very much abused for decades. Most states are still doing nothing about it, and taxation through citation continues in most jurisdictions. Is it not time to stop this universal "pocket picking?"

Chapter 17
Who Is Right?

In all that has been said or written about Liberty and the great American experiment, many eternal principles can be pointed out as beams of support for perpetuating such priceless commodities. These principles of selfless service include love for God and family, the nobility of defending those who are incapable of defending themselves, standing for what's right especially when it is not popular or politically expedient. What principles are involved in **not** standing for America? Selfishness, greed, going along to get along, ignorance, apathy, political deal making, and an overall abundance of cowardice. So, who's right? If you've gotten this far in the book you clearly know the answer. We need heroic pioneers. A pioneer is a front-runner, one who prepares the way, breaks new ground and has the courage to go where no one has dared.

Sheriff Gillespie in Clark County, NV claimed he had no authority to interfere with the BLM destroying the last ranch in his county. Gillespie essentially opined that he had no authority to keep his oath of office, that he had no authority to keep the peace, no authority to protect the lives and property of his people, and no authority to keep his word. Was he right? (Read all about that in a later chapter dedicated to the Bundy Ranch siege.)

On the other hand, in 1994 seven American sheriffs sued the Clinton administration to stop the overreach and utter despotism associated with the Brady bill. Seven out of 3086 sheriffs stood and risked their lives and careers to push the feds back where they belonged. Seven! Ultimately, this historic case (the first and only time sheriffs ever sued the federal government and won) went all the way to the U.S. Supreme Court where these pioneer sheriffs won a landmark decision, perhaps the most powerful Tenth Amendment ruling in American history. Who was right? The 3079 who did nothing or the seven who fought? The Supreme Court agreed with the seven. But even if they hadn't; would that have made the battle wrong or unworthy? Is victory the only measure of right and wrong? Courage comes in the face of the storm, not fair weather. Facing Goliath has never been easy; it was no picnic David ventured upon! But the liberty of his people was at stake! Sound familiar? If David had lost, his cause and effort would have nevertheless been the right thing to do; it would have still been worth the try. The politician will carefully and selfishly calculate each move he or she makes, attempting to ascertain the benefits to their careers before acting. The statesman weighs the principles involved and stands accordingly in defense of God, family, country, and his fellow man.

Who's right? The overwhelming majority of sheriffs and public officials who allow the EPA, FDA, BLM, etc. to come into their counties and victimize the people, or Sheriff Rogers in Elkhart County, Indiana who stood and defended an Amish farmer from the bureaucratic harassment of the Food and Drug Administration (FDA)?

On July 2, 2014, Sheriff Julian Whittington of Bossier Parish, Louisiana, took a lot of heat from some politicians and anti-religious rights groups because he supported and planned to pray at a 4th of July event in his parish. In response to the complaints Sheriff Whittington told the Shreveport Times the following:

> **I am an elected official. I'm also a citizen here. I think this is what's best for us. I don't work for anybody in Washington. What they do, what they say, I couldn't really care less.**

Sheriff Whittington is absolutely correct! So if he is, then why don't more chiefs and sheriffs defend local norms and autonomy instead of allowing hate groups to run their affairs?

Throughout world history when *anything* of significance happened; was the hero ever found within the mainstream? Are real heroes politically correct? If the Thirteen Colonies had lost the Revolutionary War, the courageous Founders of our country would have been hung as traitors and criminals. History would have recorded them as evil, horrible, extremists, and *controversial!*

Who is right? Sheriff David Clarke who has encouraged his people to be armed, or the thousands of law enforcement officials who side with gun control? Is Clarke wrong? Or does he know the truth that **gun control is against the law in America** and as such, he stands to enforce the law *and* help his constituents. Any cop (liberal or conservative, democrat or republican, or anything in between) knows that police cannot and will not be to your home in time to stop an attack. So why do so many pretend that you'll be safer if you are unarmed? Sheriff Clarke is one of the leaders in this country who refuses to be a part of such propaganda. He has told the truth! Among our nation's police, who is right; Sheriff Clarke or the hundreds of other law enforcement leaders (including Edward A. Flynn, Milwaukee City Chief of Police) who pretend to the public that gun control will keep citizens and cops safer?

They are on opposite sides of this issue, and quite frankly, opposite sides of the law! They both can't be right. So, which one is it? Which one is the "David?"

Liberty in Liberty County, Florida!

Another example of being right and standing for the truth was Liberty County Sheriff Nick Finch. On March 8, 2013 Sheriff Finch nullified the arrest of a citizen in his county, one Floyd Parrish. Parrish had been arrested by a deputy who worked for Finch. What was the crime that Parrish had been arrested for? The crook had a gun in his pocket! Was he a prohibited felon? No. Was he planning an assault or robbery? No. Parrish was driving home, that's it. Driving home! The deputy pulled Parrish over for a minor traffic violation and before Parrish knew what was going on, he was pulled out of his car and frisked. Now a real crime had been committed, but not by Mr. Parrish. The establishment would have us believe we were all protected, and Floyd Parrish needed to go to jail because he had no permit (permission slip) from the state to have a concealed gun.

Sheriff Finch did not like the lack of probable cause for the stop and certainly did not like the fact that a law-abiding citizen was going to jail for merely having a gun in his pocket. Sheriff Finch released Parrish, nullified the arrest, dropped the charges, and advised Parrish to get a permit. Done? Not even close! The deputy got his little feelings hurt when his boss would not let him keep the law-abiding citizen in jail and went crying to the State Police. The Police State conducted an investigation on Finch for "destroying public documents" and three months later – you guessed it, arrested Sheriff Finch and booked him into his own jail! He was released without bail. But "conservative" Florida Governor Rick Scott took it upon himself to remove Finch from office and put one of the State Police in as Liberty County Sheriff the next day. So, now Finch had no salary and no way to pay for his defense. Finch was up the proverbial creek.

Luckily, the story began spreading online, and the people of America began donating to help with his legal fees. No, the National Sheriffs' Association did not help and neither did the Florida Sheriffs' Association. Oath Keepers and CSPOA did help him as well as a lot of other patriotic individuals.

Sheriff Finch was charged with one felony and one misdemeanor for his "heinous" act of releasing Mr Parrish.

The State also re-arrested Mr. Parrish, then released him just as Finch had done, but charged him $300 for their trouble! (It's always about the money!)

Willie Megs, the prosecutor in this case, offered Finch a plea deal; just leave office and all charges will be dropped! Finch refused and went to court. He knew the whole thing was stupid, bogus and frivolous. He counted on the jury of his peers recognizing that, too. They did! They took 75 minutes to find Sheriff Nick Finch not guilty on all charges. He was restored to his position in a matter of minutes.

One key point during the trial was when Sheriff Finch took the stand and the prosecutor badgered him about how he thought he was above the law. After a monotonous barrage of the same questions and attacks creatively disguised over and over, Sheriff Finch confidently looked the prosecutor and the jury in the eye and said, "At some point, the Constitution has to count for something." One of the most powerful statements ever made by any peace officer from the witness stand in American history. Sheriff Finch boldly defended his oath of office and the Second Amendment in a court of law. He stood for what's right, he stood for the Constitution, and for the "little guy" against the system that no longer serves the people.

Who was right; Sheriff Finch or the deputy and the State? Jefferson called laws "the tools of the tyrant." It certainly would appear he was right! If a citizen has wronged no one, has threatened no one and done nothing to harm another living soul, why should that citizen go to jail? Concealed carry laws are nothing more than the perpetuation of gun control; you know, touching one of those untouchable rights that *shall not be infringed.* Are the police who enforce such laws right, or was Sheriff Finch right?

Thankfully, there are some others besides sheriffs catching on to the principles of freedom, interposition and state sovereignty. Oklahoma Governor Mary Fallin recently signed legislation exempting the state from the federal government's Common Core, which is the Dept. of Education's version of No Child Left Behind part II. Governor Fallin and the State's legislature overwhelmingly said, not in *their* state!

Governor Butch Otter of Idaho signed similar legislation essentially nullifying all federal gun control laws! Furthermore, this legislation makes it a crime to have any State officers or any from its political subdivisions cooperate in any manner with federal gun laws! As part of its justification for enacting this courageous state law, Idaho referred to the Mack/Printz case which contains what has become known as the "anti-commandeering doctrine." (The feds cannot commandeer state officials to enforce federal statutes.)

So again; who's right? The many excuse-makers who say the federal government trumps the states in everything or these two states and their governors? Let's look at it one more time:

...State legislatures are not subject to federal direction.

~ Justice Scalia, Mack/Printz v US

Governors Otto and Fallin know it and many others are catching on. Indiana and South Carolina have passed similar legislation and Governor Perry in Texas has already told the feds that they will not be "commandeering" land along the Red River as they recently announced they intended to do. It's amazing how much freedom can be safeguarded when you have a few "Davids" standing against Goliath!

In a story by World Net Daily, Sheriff John Cooke of Weld County, Colorado, in response to dozens of Colorado sheriffs standing against the state's new gun laws, said, "Even the federal courts cannot make me enforce the laws. So, if we lose and the judge says, 'No, these laws *are* constitutional,' I still set the priorities and the resources for my agency. There's no law in the state of Colorado that says I have to enforce the law, so I still won't enforce them, because in my belief and in my opinion, it's not my job to turn law-abiding gun owners into criminals."

This is precisely what the people of this country yearn for, and taking stands like Sheriff Cooke has done is absolutely what this book is about: principle before politics and liberty before anything else. God's law of "doing unto others" and in doing good to all mankind, being fair and protecting justice. Is this not what these aforementioned hero sheriffs have done? Absolutely! Are you with them?

Chapter 18
The January 2014 CSPOA Resolution

The January 2014 CSPOA conference began with a prayer. Right then, any newcomers could tell there would be something different about this meeting of over 75 sheriffs, police chiefs, peace officers and other elected officials and public servants from 31 different states. As the day progressed, each of the speakers noted God's role in our task; how could they not? It takes faith to understand freedom; it takes more than courage to stand when the tide is going against you. A self-serving person will go with the flow, but a person of principle – a person of faith – stands even when he or she stands alone against the crashing waves.

The men and women at this conference did not attend out of any desire to make their lives easier or to make themselves more popular. They came because their beliefs demanded that they be there. Every day they pledge their lives, their fortunes and their sacred honor for a cause they believe in: The Holy Cause of Liberty. The same pledge that guided our Founding Fathers as they wrote The Declaration of Independence, The U.S. Constitution and the Bill of Rights.

One of our primary goals was to draft a resolution that would state clearly how we felt about the current abuses raining down from the Federal government, and to establish boundaries and guidelines for federal agents and employees to follow when entering local jurisdictions. We spent the early afternoon discussing this document, and the tone in the room was nothing short of miraculous. There was some discussion about proper wording, but there was no real disagreement on what we wanted to say. There were some who worried that if the document was worded too strongly others would be hesitant to join us, but there were none who said it was too strongly worded for themselves. There were no lost tempers; no heated arguments. Nobody walked out of the room in anger. How is this possible in a room full of strong-willed, independent sheriffs from across the nation? There's only one answer. They were of one heart and one mind, and they were acting in courage with the strength of faith.

After the finished resolution was read back to the group, we felt another prayer was needed. We prayed over this document, that it could touch the hearts and minds of many other sheriffs, peace officers, public officials and citizens across the nation; that it could be an instrument used to restore liberty to countless numbers who are losing it a little more each day. We prayed that it could be taken in the spirit that it was written: Not a spirit of anger or violence, but a spirit of peace and freedom. We prayed that it could be a clarion call to unite the good people across the nation who want to stand, but do not want to stand alone.

We hope as you read this document that you will be led to stand with us, that we can totally commit to save this nation and people that we love, remembering that faith is a strength our adversary can neither possess nor comprehend.

Resolution Drafted by the Constitutional Sheriffs and Peace Officers Association

Pursuant to the powers and duties bestowed upon us by our citizens, the undersigned do hereby resolve that any Federal officer, agent, or employee, regardless of supposed congressional authorization, is required to obey and observe limitations consisting of the enumerated powers as detailed within Article 1 Section 8 of the U S Constitution and the Bill Of Rights.

The people of these united States are, and have a right to be, free and independent, and these rights are derived from the "Laws of Nature and Nature's God." As such, they must be free from infringements on the right to keep and bear arms, unreasonable searches and seizures, capricious detainments and infringements on every other natural right whether enumerated or not. (9th amendment)

We further reaffirm that "The powers not delegated to the United States by the Constitution, nor prohibited by it to the states, are reserved to the states respectively, or to the people." (10th amendment)

Furthermore, we maintain that no agency established by the U S Congress can develop its own policies or regulations which supersede the Bill of Rights or the Constitution, nor does the executive branch have the power to make law, overturn law or set aside law.

Therefore, in order to protect the American people, BE IT RESOLVED THAT, The following abuses will not be allowed or tolerated:

1. Registration of personal firearms under any circumstances.
2. Confiscation of firearms without probable cause, due process, and constitutionally compliant warrants issued by a local or state jurisdiction.
3. Audits or searches of a citizen's personal affairs or finances without probable cause, and due process, and constitutionally compliant warrants issued by a local or state jurisdiction.
4. Inspections of person or property without probable cause and constitutionally compliant warrants as required by the 4th Amendment and issued by a local or state jurisdiction.

5. The detainment or search of citizens without probable cause and proper due process compliance, or the informed consent of the citizen.
6. Arrests with continued incarcerations without charges and complete due process, including, but not limited to public and speedy jury trials, in a court of state or local jurisdiction.
7. Domestic utilization of our nation's military or federal agencies operating under power granted under the laws of war against American citizens.
8. Arrest of citizens or seizure of persons or property without first notifying and obtaining the express consent of the local sheriff.

AND, BE IT FURTHER RESOLVED,
that the undersigned Sheriffs, Peace Officers, Public Servants and citizens, do hereby denounce any acts or agencies which promote the aforementioned practices. All actions by the Federal Government and its agents will conform strictly and implicitly with the principles expressed within the United States Constitution, Declaration of Independence, and the Bill of Rights.

There is no greater obligation or responsibility of any government officer than to protect the rights of the people. Thus, any conduct contrary to the United States Constitution, Declaration of Independence, or the Bill of Rights will be dealt with as criminal activity.

The real point of this resolution is a very simple one; the federal government should follow the Constitution, obey it and live by the principles listed therein. Sheriffs and chiefs of police likewise should exercise some leadership and put the feds on notice that they expect federal agents to follow the Constitution when they enter their jurisdictions. It is only fair and proper to serve due notice to the feds that *IF* they intend to conduct door-to-door gun confiscations, or seize cattle or bank accounts, or make arrests, that local law enforcement leaders will stand in the way and do all they can to prevent such abuse.

If Sheriff Gillespie had moved 200 of his deputies into Bunkerville, Nevada and ordered the feds to stand down, we would have never heard of Cliven Bundy! To let federal bureaucracies know that their overreach, heavy handed tactics, and illegal activity will not be tolerated is the best way to avoid such problems in the future. If hundreds of sheriffs and chiefs were united in this effort, this would be the ultimate state-of-the-art crime prevention program, and these sorts of incidents would decrease exponentially, or perhaps even disappear. Isn't that what we want? It would be much better than simply sitting back and waiting for the next volatile or violent standoff to occur. Make no mistake about it; they will happen again! Would you rather prevent them or wait until it lands in your town?

County by county, Craven County!

We're proud to have the Craven County, North Carolina Republican Party stand with us!

Resolution of Support for the Constitutional Sheriffs and Peace Officers Association's January 24, 2014 Resolution which Upholds and Supports The United States Constitution and the Bill of Rights

Whereas, the United States Constitution and the Bill of Rights are the supreme law of the land; and

Whereas, the rights enshrined in the Constitution and Bill of Rights are derived from God and cannot be superseded by the act of any agency's regulatory action; and

Whereas, the Powers not expressly granted to the Federal Government by the Constitution are reserved for the States and the People; and

Whereas, the Executive Branch does not have the right to make law, overturn law, or set aside law.

Resolved, That the Craven County Republican Party supports the Resolution passed by the Constitutional Sheriffs and Peace Officers Association on January 24, 2014 (CSPOA Resolution attached). This resolution sets forth 8 abuses of Constitutional Rights that will not be tolerated and obligates Sheriffs to oppose and arrest any Federal authorities who attempt to deny Constitutional Rights of American Citizens.

This is a great start, and we need many more like them. When we have Republicans (and hopefully Democrats and all others) standing for liberty and these efforts are supported by governors, sheriffs, cops, and all local officials there will be no stopping it! We will take America back!

Chapter 19
The Bundy Ranch Siege

Cliven Bundy and his family (all 14 children) stood against unspeakable odds (Goliath) and fought to maintain the family's livelihood: the ranch that had been in the family for decades. The Bundys were the last ranchers to survive the treachery of the federal bureaucrats hell-bent on destroying all ranching in Nevada. Fifty-two other ranchers had been forced off the land and out of business in Clark County alone. Clive Bundy warned the other ranchers not to sign the "new deal" with the BLM (Bureau of Land Management) that represented a better and easier contract for water rights and usage. Bundy was right. The new contract proved to be a trap and suckered the other ranchers into a deal that cost hundreds of jobs and family businesses, not to mention the damage it did to the nation's food supply.

The Bundy stand off took on a life of its own and received a great deal of media coverage. Much of what aired was slanted, and at times it was downright pro-government propaganda. I have known the Bundys personally for a number of years, and knew what kind of people they were, and was shocked to discover that the federal government was willing and ready to kill the Bundys and other protesters over the issue of cows eating grass on public lands. (The only thing the feds intended for these "public" lands was to make certain the public had no access to them.) The Bundys wanted merely to be left alone to raise cattle and their family.

Numerous hearings in federal courts had taken place over the years and Bundy lost them all. He now faced expulsion and the confiscation of his cattle. He determined, with unanimous support from his family, to do "whatever it takes" to keep his ranch and land. Hundreds of Americans from all over the country came to stand with the Bundys.

However, to understand all that came to a head at the Bundy Ranch we need to know some background. First of all, the other ranchers did not all go down easily. The Dann sisters, who happened to be Native American, fought and lost everything!

Wayne Hage, a rancher in northern Nye County, fought the BLM and US Forest Service and he won in court. However, this fight against the federal Goliath took 25 years. Hage's wife died in 1996 and he remarried Helen Chenoweth, the former U.S. Congresswoman from Idaho. Chenoweth was a staunch fighter herself and had stood for liberty in DC and against federal intrusions and corruption. Hage and Helen eventually passed away and his children continued the battle. The following is their story:

In an historic ruling, Chief Judge Robert C. Jones of the Federal District Court of Nevada struck a major blow for property rights and, at the same time, has smacked down federal agencies that have been riding roughshod over Western ranchers and property owners. The long-awaited ruling finally settled a 25 year legal battle that was completely ignored by the major media. *U.S. v. Hage,* **settled some key constitutional issues and proved the federal government, i.e. the BLM and USFS, had committed various crimes during this absurd quarter of a century battle.**

As previously reported in June of 2012, Judge Jones issued a scorching preliminary bench ruling that charged federal officials of the USFS and BLM with an ongoing series of illegal actions against Nevada rancher Wayne Hage that the judge described as *"abhorrent"* **and** *a literal, criminal conspiracy.*

Judge Jones said he found that "the government and the agents of the government in that locale, sometime in the '70s and '80s, entered into a *conspiracy,* **a literal, intentional** *conspiracy,* **to deprive the Hages of not only their grazing rights, for whatever reason, but also to deprive them of their vested property rights and I find that that's a sufficient basis to hold that there is irreparable harm if I don't … restrain the government from continuing in that conduct."**

In fact, Judge Jones accused these federal bureaucrats of racketeering under the federal RICO (Racketeer Influenced and Corruption Organizations) statute, and accused them as well of extortion, mail fraud, and fraud, in an effort "to kill the business of Mr. Hage."

The Hage family has waged a heroic decades-long legal battle against these abusive agencies, in a David vs. Goliath contest against the combined might of the U.S. Department of Justice and the BLM/USFS legal teams. Precious few regular citizens are willing to undertake such a seemingly hopeless and costly effort as to challenge the formidable power and bottomless resources of the federal government. The Bundy family, however, was determined. The lambasting the BLM took from Judge Jones did not deter them one iota and no criminal charges were ever pursued even though the Judge had requested such.

The Hages' son, Wayne N. Hage and other family members have continued ranching and have continued the legal fight. Hage hailed Judge Jones' May 24 decision as a landmark ruling for property rights, which the American Founding Fathers recognized as the bedrock of liberty and an essential security against tyrannical government.

The court found, "In the present case, the Government's actions over the past two decades shock the conscience of the Court." This finding, coupled with the court's finding that agents of the BLM and the USFS engaged in a conspiracy to deprive the Hage family of their vested property

rights, opens the door to potential lawsuits against the individual agents personally for their unconstitutional actions.

~ ~ ~

Tonopah BLM manager, Tom Seley, and Forest Ranger Steve Williams were both found to be in contempt of court, and were referred to the U.S. attorney for possible prosecution for criminal obstruction of justice.

~ ~ ~

Is this clear enough for you? The federal government committed criminal conspiracy and racketeering, violated the Hages' constitutional rights, and was held in contempt of court by a judge who said the actions of the federal agents *"shocked the conscience of the court."* Criminal activity by the BLM and USFS for over two decades and *NO ONE* in the federal government did anything about it! So now this same federal bureaucracy goes after Cliven Bundy for 20 years and again *NO ONE* does anything about it. Some even blamed the Bundys for the entire fiasco! Unbelievable! Are you going to allow this to happen in your jurisdiction? Are you going to keep asking these criminals for more federal grants and then brag how you're getting "your fair share?" There is absolutely nothing fair about it!

I went to the Bundy Ranch on April 12, 2014, accompanied by my son Jimmy, Wendy Larchick (a lawyer) and her father

Gale (a retired police officer). We all drove together from Mesa, Arizona to Bunkerville, Nevada. As we neared "ground zero" we became frustrated by the horrible stop-and-go traffic. While sitting on the I-15 freeway I received a call from one of our CSPOA members who had arrived the day before. He was on the front lines of the 150 or so crowd of men and women who were marching towards the makeshift BLM corral to free the Bundy cattle. Come what may, he and the others were determined to set the cattle free. This CSPOA member was a 15-year law enforcement veteran and understood the gravity of the situation in which he had voluntarily placed himself.

Over the phone he said, "Sheriff, these agents are going to kill us. At first, they threatened to arrest us, but now they are threatening to shoot us. There is no question in my mind, they are going to kill us. Please, just tell my wife that I love her." He abruptly hung up and I sat in my truck stunned. I told the others in the vehicle with me what he had said, and they suggested I put on my emergency blinkers and go around the stalled traffic on the right side shoulder. I did exactly that. Several highway patrol units were doing the same thing and heading to the exact place we were. The entire situation appeared worse than bleak.

When we arrived, we were met by Stewart Rhodes of Oath Keepers and we went into the ranch area with him and Lory Storm, driving her 4x4 pickup. As we approached the scene we could tell that no shooting had occurred. The word was out that the BLM and their hired mercenaries were leaving. No one really knew why. My CSPOA contact said the military weaponry was there, the shooters were ready and had given warnings of the impending attack and then suddenly, they stood down. Some said the Clark county sheriff brokered a deal with them, after stating for weeks that he had *"no authority to interfere."* Others had stated that the women up at the front of the marchers had forced the would-be shooters to back off. Others said it was just a miracle. In fact, quite a few said that.

There were approximately 600 to 700 supporters surrounding the area where the cows were now being set free. I was asked to help with crowd control as some of the hero cowboys and cowgirls were worried that too many people near the cattle might spook them and cause a stampede. The crowd totally cooperated. As the captive cattle came out and trotted along the ravine just under the I-15 overpass, a feeling of reverence swept over the entire crowd. You could have heard a pin drop on the desert sand! It was among the most sacred, solemn, patriotic moments of my life. Most had tears swelling in their eyes or rolling down their cheeks. As the last animal crossed over to freedom, we all started hugging each other. My son hugged me with tears in his eyes and the rest of us, mostly total strangers, embraced as the spirit of liberty overwhelmed us. I imagine we felt the same as the Founding Fathers did when they knew they had been spared by the hand of God against overwhelming odds.

After we rode back to the stage location several reporters asked me for an interview. My heart was still full and my eyes still moist. I told them about the brave women who were there at the Bundy Ranch, putting themselves in harm's way for freedom and the Bundys. The women had indeed put themselves in front with the men and I was trying to honor them for their bravery. Clearly, if the feds had started shooting at the crowd, they would have killed unarmed men and women, just like at Waco and Ruby Ridge. Please remember that my main purpose in going to the Bundy Ranch, was to see that we stood strong, yet peacefully, and that the situation did not escalate to violence. I didn't want to see **anybody** get shot; men, women, protesters or feds!

Anyway, in case you're still on the fence about this whole affair, let me make it perfectly clear that putting the women at the front was never planned by anyone. The women just did it because they felt it was the right thing to do, and they were not afraid. Not at any time did the Bundy family or anyone else at the scene make any suggestion to use women as shields or to put them in front, and **the word 'children' was never used, except by the media!**

I was impressed with all the women who participated that day and what they did to stand for liberty. I want to give them credit for a peaceful resolution in a volatile life-and-death situation. We would not have made it without them! I have never stood with such great people and I will never forget this most powerful and patriotic moment.

The Hage case was not exactly the same as the Bundy battle, but there were legal and constitutional similarities. The most glaring ones being the never-ending dogged determination by the government to ruin the lives and businesses of these ranchers and the criminal acts by our own federal government. Another despicable coincidence; *NO ONE* in Washington lifted a finger to help or defend the Hages or the Bundys. The Hages, however, had a constitutional Sheriff, Sheriff Tony DeMeo who in fact intervened, interfered, and interposed (put himself in the way) on behalf of the victims, the Hage family, and stopped the confiscation of the Hage cattle. The BLM agents even threatened Sheriff DeMeo that they would return, of course, with their SWAT team. Sheriff DeMeo told the feds, Go ahead; I've got one, too!

Therein lies the huge difference between the Hage case and the Bundy case; one had a constitutional Sheriff with the courage to do his job, and the Bundys had, well, the opposite! There were some heroes at Bunkerville, and Cliven Bundy and his family were certainly heroes. The people who traveled from all across the country to stand with their neighbors (the Bundys) were heroes. The cowboys and cowgirls who brought the cows home were heroes, and one Deputy Sheriff, Tom Roberts was a hero. He interposed and stopped a horrible tragedy.

Has anyone been transparent in DC, the White House, or the halls of Congress regarding this entire fiasco? Why don't these "leaders" tell us how much money they spent to go after the Bundys and who they hired as hit men at the scene and how much it cost the American taxpayers to do so? The actions of the federal government were never, at any time during this entire episode, honorable, lawful, or appropriate police behavior. Governor Sandoval assailed the feds for violating the Constitution with their make-shift freedom of speech corral, yet he did nothing about it! He allowed the feds to threaten violence and arrest to Nevadans who did not obey the BLM rules about freedom of speech. It was up to the whims of federal bureaucrats how, when, and where they got to exercise their right to freedom of speech.

But is this not the same as what they're doing to the Second Amendment? The government tells us how we can keep and bear arms, they tell us where we can keep and bear arms, they tell us how many guns we can have, how much ammo we can have, and if we make a mistake they send us to jail, plunder our substance, and label us terrorists! All this regarding *rights* that are guaranteed in our Constitution. Rights our sheriffs and peace officers are sworn to defend and protect. One kept his oath that day. It was not the governor, it was not the sheriff, it was not a U.S. senator; none of them did! It was a deputy sheriff.

The following is a press release from the Bundy family:

As we have had the opportunity to reflect on the events that took place between March 26th and April 12th, 2014—we have experienced feelings of concern, confusion, fear, anger, sadness and joy. Our peaceful community has been shaken. In many ways, we are still processing the magnitude of what took place. We ask ourselves so many questions; did the federal government really come into this valley and terrorize our community? Did hundreds of armed forces, in Red Dawn fashion, lock down the hills and valleys of our peaceful home—threatening at gunpoint, anyone who stepped off the paved road, with forceful and lethal action? Did we really see armed forces convoying through the streets of our town, diligently recording names and identities of anyone who glanced wrong or opposed them in any way? Was there really heavy equipment in the form of dump trucks and backhoes, on our mountains, tearing up infrastructure that we have used for hundreds of years, and is vital to our survival? Were we truly in the crosshairs of snipers, and under surveillance by the latest in technological weapons? Did these forces actually point their rifles in the faces of our little children, while beating their unarmed fathers to the dirt and hauling them off in chains? Did they really body-slam our friend, a 59 year old woman to the ground, and sic German Shepherds on our neighbors—even a pregnant woman? Did they actually shock a man multiple times with a 50,000 volt Taser for honorably protecting his aunt, while she gathered herself out of the dust? We reflect in sadness and awe that this could take place in our little town.

The terror of armed men occupying our land will never be forgotten. The feelings of despair of these events will long reside in our hearts. Thoughts of anxiousness that this may ever happen again, will awaken us from our pillows from time to time. During quiet reflection, we may ask ourselves if we did the right thing by resisting. Were we in the right when we acted to safeguard ourselves? When the only response to our multiple pleas for help was silence, when we were left alone to clean our cuts and wounds, did we have a divine right, duty, and obligation to protect our family and ourselves? We recall the many times we pleaded with our local government to protect us; the numerous times we called 911, and begged our Sheriff to send his deputies to assist. Our cries of distress were met with silence. We ask ourselves, "Did we try hard enough to get our local government and law enforcement to act as a buffer and perform their duty to protect and serve?" Were the hundreds of phone calls not enough, or is it just that our elected leaders and Sheriff have forsaken the people in trade for power and money? We whole-heartedly want to believe that our Sheriff would not abandon us, but where has his shielding influence been? Why was he not here to represent and protect the very men, women and children of his county that he swore an oath for? Why did he stand silent and neutral, knowing our community was in terror? What was his motivation of inaction; was it fear of the federal government or political reprisal from powerful politicians?

The scars of this traumatic event will heal over time. We hope our community will eventually return to a sense of normalcy. We fervently hope and pray that these heavy-handed tactics will not be used on us or any other American ever again. We wonder if our hopes will be in vain; will they return? Will they come back with greater force and more cunning tactics than before? Will our Sheriff keep his oath this time, and use his lawful forces to stop them, or will the people be left to their own protection? Will the good people of this nation yet again have to come running to the rescue of a neighbor? Will veterans, retired police force, churches, businesses, families and individuals have to unite once again to confront these acts of governmental terror upon the American people? Will our local government rouse themselves from disaffection and intervene—protecting the people? Will they stop fearing to do the right thing and come to the realization that the people are more important than a government agency? Will they fight for the rights of the state and her people? They must stop putting personal gain and advancement in front of the rights of citizens. They need to recognize, that as our elected representatives, they have more power than those governing in brute force, as they have the might of the people of this state backing them. With that power we invest in them, they have the obligation to safeguard our livelihoods, combat forces of fear, and protect our lives with their own.

A few weeks ago, our community was in a state of innocence and naivety. We felt safe and mostly kept to ourselves. We thought the world's problems would only affect us through television, and could be shut off with the push of a button. Our innocence has left us now, we have experienced first-hand the breath of force upon our necks. We have gasped in desperation as our lives and agency were threatened. Our cries have been ignored by our guardians in the next room. We faced a choice—either lie down and submit helplessly in defeat, or bite, scratch, and fight until help would come. We are eternally and profoundly grateful for the many heroic neighbors who heard our desperate cries and crashed through the windows to rescue. We additionally thank the thousands that came from every State in this great nation, and stood in front of raised guns in our defense, and for the hope that those same guns would never come to their doors and their families. We are grateful for those that arrived with pen and camera, those that arrived with faith and prayers, and those that arrived with fist and gun. The variety of support from all walks of life has shown that this was an event that truly touched the good hearts of many Americans. We cannot thank you all enough—you have restored our faith in the goodness of the

American people.

Our message to all, is that it is time to make things right. It is time to adhere to the supreme law of the land—The Constitution of the United States. It is time to understand right, stand for what's right, and do whatever it takes to make it right. We must continue the vision of our Founding Fathers in preserving the freedoms of the American people and the sovereign rights of the States. A nation can never abdicate its fate to an authority it cannot control. Men must decide if their rights and freedoms are God-granted or are assigned by a federal government. We believe in the rule of law and sustain a limited government. May God bless us to protect this sacred instrument.

Clark County Sheriff Doug Gillespie said he had no authority to interfere and referred the Bundys and all other concerned citizens to the BLM. The Bundys did not need to be referred to the BLM, they were already surrounded by them! Nevertheless, Gillespie's cowardice and lack of knowledge of his own job are strikingly scary as he claimed to his constituents that he had no authority to keep his oath of office, had no authority to keep the peace, and ultimately had no authority to *protect* life and *serve* the people of his jurisdiction!

Then on June 5, 2014, as reported by *The Las Vegas Review Journal*, Sheriff Doug Gillespie doubled down on his ineptness and malfeasance by blaming the entire Bundy Ranch fiasco on the Bundys and the BLM! Now Gillespie is claiming that the BLM lied to him and the BLM is saying the same about the Sheriff. However, the Sheriff is saying that

Bundy "allowed" all his supporters from across the country to descend upon his ranch and aim guns at law enforcement. "They need to be held accountable for it," Sheriff Gillespie said authoritatively! Even the BLM in a press release by spokeswoman Celia Boddington, claimed that Sheriff Gillespie had agreed to be at the Bundy Ranch to control the crowd of protesters.

Amazing isn't it? The BLM claims the Sheriff did not do his job and the Sheriff claims the BLM lied! Wow, they are both right! And the two points together are precisely what caused the horrible situation in the first place. If Sheriff Gillespie truly wants accountability, then he should start with his own and then investigate all the crimes committed by the BLM. That would be the only way in which **true accountability** could ever be achieved.

Richard Mack | *Are You A David?*

Chapter 20
Boozers, Barbers and Pumpkin Festivals

The dearth of leadership and appropriate training in dealing with the public is far too widespread. A lack of belief in fundamental principles by our nation's law enforcement leaders is a huge part of the problem. A problem exacerbated by the SWAT mentality of the American police community.

The following excerpts are from an article entitled "Cops or Soldiers" in the March 22nd, 2014 issue of The Economist.

Peter Kraska, a professor at Eastern Kentucky University's School of Justice Studies, estimates that

SWAT teams were deployed about 3,000 times in 1980 but are now used around 50,000 times a year. (John Whitehead, in his book *A Government of Wolves: The Emerging American Police State* estimates 80,000 total police raids per year.) Some cities use SWAT teams for routine patrols in high-crime areas. Baltimore and Dallas have used them to break up poker games. In 2010, the city of New Haven, Connecticut sent a SWAT team to a bar suspected of serving under-age drinkers. That same year heavily-armed police raided barber shops around Orlando, Florida; they said they were hunting for guns and drugs but ended up arresting 34 people for "barbering without a license."

~ ~ ~

According to Mr. Kraska, most SWAT deployments are not in response to violent, life-threatening crimes, but to serve drug-related warrants in private homes.

He estimates that 89% of police departments serving American cities with more than 50,000 people had SWAT teams in the late 1990s—almost double the level in the mid-1980s. By 2007 more than 80% of police departments in cities with between 25,000 and 50,000 people had them, up from 20% in the mid-1980s (there are around 18,000 state and local police agencies in America, compared with fewer than 100 in Britain).

The number of SWAT deployments soared even as

violent crime fell. And although in recent years crime rates have risen in smaller American cities, Mr Kraska writes that the rise in small-town SWAT teams was driven not by need, but by fear of being left behind. Fred Leland, a police lieutenant in the small town of Walpole, Massachusetts, says that police departments in towns like his often invest in military-style kit because they "want to keep up" with larger forces.

~ ~ ~

Big grants for big guns!

Federal cash—first to wage war on drugs, then on terror—has paid for much of the heavy weaponry used by SWAT teams. Between 2002 and 2011 the Department of Homeland Security disbursed $35 billion in grants to state and local police. Also, the Pentagon offers surplus military kit to police departments. According to Mr Balko, by 2005 it had provided such gear to more than 17,000 law-enforcement agencies.

These programmes provide useful defensive equipment, such as body armor and helmets. But it is hard to see why Fargo, North Dakota—a city that averages fewer than two murders a year—needs an armored personnel-carrier with a rotating turret. Keene, a small town in New Hampshire which had three homicides between 1999 and 2012, spent nearly $286,000 on an armored personnel carrier known as a BearCat. The local police chief said it would be used to patrol Keene's "Pumpkin Festival and other dangerous situations". A Reason-Rupe poll found that 58% of Americans think the use of drones, military weapons and armored vehicles by the police has gone "too far".

Because of a legal quirk, SWAT raids can be profitable. Rules on civil asset-forfeiture allow the police to seize anything which they can plausibly claim was the proceeds of a crime. Crucially, the property-owner need not be convicted of that crime. If the police find drugs in his house, they can take his cash and possibly the house, too. He must sue to get them back.

Many police departments now depend on forfeiture for a fat chunk of their budgets. In 1986, its first year of operation, the federal Asset Forfeiture Fund held $93.7m. By 2012, that and the related Seized Asset Deposit Fund held nearly $6 billion.

Mr Balko contends that these forfeiture laws are "unfair on a very basic level." They "disproportionately affect low-income people" and provide a perverse incentive for police to focus on drug-related crimes, which "come with a potential kickback to the police department," rather than rape and murder investigations, which do not. They also provide an incentive to arrest suspected drug-dealers inside their houses, which can be seized, and to bust stash houses after most of their drugs have been sold, when police can seize the cash.
Kara Dansky of the American Civil Liberties Union,

who is overseeing a study into police militarization, notices a more martial tone in recent years in the materials used to recruit and train new police officers. A recruiting video in Newport Beach, California, for instance, shows officers loading assault rifles, firing weapons, chasing suspects, putting people in headlocks and releasing snarling dogs.

This is no doubt sexier than showing them poring over paperwork or attending a neighborhood-watch meeting. But does it attract the right sort of recruit, or foster the right attitude among serving officers? Mr Balko cites the T-shirts that some off-duty cops wear as evidence of a culture that celebrates violence ("We get up early to beat the crowds"; "You huff and you puff and we'll blow your door down").

Others retort that Mr Balko and his allies rely too much on cherry-picked examples of raids gone wrong. Tragic accidents happen and some police departments use their SWAT teams badly, but most use them well, says Lance Eldridge, a former army officer and ex-sheriff's deputy in Colorado.

It would be easier to determine who is right if police departments released more information about how and how often they deploy SWAT teams. But most are extremely cagey. In 2009 Maryland's governor, Martin O'Malley, signed a law requiring the police in his state to report such information every six months. Three published reports showed that SWAT teams were most often deployed to serve search warrants on people suspected of crimes involving drugs and other contraband, but the law is set to expire this year. Utah's legislature has passed a similar measure; it awaits the governor's signature.

No one wants to eliminate SWAT teams. Imminent threats to human life require a swift, forceful response. That, say critics, is what SWAT teams should be used for: not for serving warrants on people suspected of nonviolent crimes, breaking up poker games or seeing that the Pumpkin Festival doesn't get out of hand.

Chapter 21
What If It's True?

Truly we are living in "the best of times and the worst of times." We enjoy so much that other generations have not had, and yet we are on the brink of losing it all. If you'll pardon me a very wide poetic license, we could even call this book the "Tale of Two Sheriffs." I've said much about the brave men and women who are standing and much about those who are not.

We will never win **IF** we don't know ourselves and thereby gain the ability to assess our own personal integrity, our oaths of office, our honor and our duty to help our neighbors. Likewise, we must know our enemy and understand the threat to America. If we don't know who the enemy is there is no way to defeat him! Complete destruction and defeat is inevitable if we do not recognize **what** is happening and **who** is doing it. Then after we "see and hear" what is actually occurring, we must have the courage to interpose, intervene, and interfere! Which sheriff or peace officer are you and which one do your people want and deserve?

Many people across America purchased *The County Sheriff: America's Last Hope* in hopes that their Sheriff would read it and perhaps realize the extent of their power and responsibility to "serve and protect." In fact, we launched a campaign which we humorously called "No Sheriff Left Behind" and got one of these books into the hands of every sheriff in America. But the old adage of "you can lead a [sheriff] to water, but you can't make him [keep his oath]" certainly applies here. It's more than regrettable that the people who need to read this book the most will more than likely never pick it up. It might be analogous to the children of Israel who only had to look upon the snake at the top of the pole in order to be healed of deadly poison. Many rationalized that it was just too easy and therefore, such an innocuous act could never cure them.

It is the same today. Many will make the excuses that liberty cannot be restored pursuant to the "county by county" formula described herein; that would be too easy! If we fail to fight now when the battle could be relatively simple, then how could we ever imagine fighting later when the possibility for victory will be drastically diminished? The question now is one of awful moment to our country. You county commissioners, county supervisors, mayors, city councils, state representatives/senators, governors, and sheriffs; your people have every right to know: will you stand for liberty?

A sheriff in New Mexico said he could be arrested if he did. All the excuses have been heard repeatedly and addressed in this book. Now, no more excuses, murmuring or whining. Will you stand for liberty?

This book has pointed out ubiquitous corruption and criminality of our own government. The existence of it all is absolutely undeniable! We know that there is no line the Federal Government will not cross, no parameter they will not breach, no law they will not break! Therefore, the only question remaining is; what will we do about it?

What if it is true? What if the people of this country, and especially in your county or town, could have their freedom back? And what if you could give it back to them? Is there anything you would not do to make this dream come true? You completely and entirely possess the power to restore the American Dream. The American Dream, the precious gift of Liberty, you have the power to give it back!

As previously expressed herein, some have claimed that nobility exists in support of corruption and the movement to destroy our Constitution. No, within this mainstream river of corruption, there lives no honor or nobility, no heroes. If we are to return to the precious principles that God Almighty gave us as His children, then we must turn ourselves and our hearts back! The answer is behind us, it's in our history and our foundation. It will not be found in *"moving forward!"*

The solution will be found if we go back to those principles of equality, being our brother's keepers, the golden rule, and the rule of law.

No, the Constitution will never protect you. It will not stop tyranny or corruption or the criminality of government agents. But *YOU* can! The Constitution can only protect us *IF* we have someone willing to enforce it! Otherwise, the Constitution sits as a piece of paper in some museum in Washington DC!

You can interpose, enforce the law, keep your oath, and protect and serve. When government becomes "venal and oppressive," to whom can the people turn for peace, safety, freedom, and protection? Should they not be able to turn to the very leaders in their communities who they hired to keep the peace? The very officials who were granted stewardship over the land? You are the stewards of liberty, the guards of the Constitution! When the people need you the most, how can you possibly turn your back?

You are the good shepherd; you are in a position to be *David*, ready and willing to take on Goliath, no matter where he comes from, no matter what the consequences! What if it's true? What if there really is a *chance* that you could literally restore freedom in your hometown? Would you not at least want to try? Would you now, when America needs you the most, shun the fight? If it is true that you could save your people from tyranny, wouldn't liberty be worth it?

Now, after all the analysis and exposure of the demise of America and its destruction from within; what is the final tribute and testimony of this book? Let it be the final words uttered by Stephen Emil Porak, United States Marine, Patriot, Teacher and Man of Honor. Leaving this life on March 4, 2014 after a battle with cancer, he asked that the following message be delivered to you all:

> **Tell the Sheriffs of this great country, tell them that it's true; they can save America!**

Let the message go out, let liberty be proclaimed throughout all the land, let go of your fears and excuses. Stand and courageously, *answer the call!*

You Are The David!

Richard Mack | *Are You A David?*

About the Author
Sheriff Richard Mack (Ret)

Sheriff Mack: lawman, detective, undercover narcotics agent, author, consultant, activist, motivational speaker, and crusader for liberty, has had a very storied career. Mack is the son of an FBI agent and began his own law enforcement career as a street cop in Provo, Utah. After graduating from BYU in 1978, Mack became an officer with Provo P. D. He was soon promoted to corporal, sergeant, and detective.

Eleven years later Mack moved home to Arizona where he ran for sheriff. He was elected Graham County Sheriff and served as such for eight years. In 1994 federal agents informed all sheriffs that they would be required to participate in a gun control scheme known as the Brady Bill. Mack refused and became the first sheriff in American history to sue the Federal Government and win a landmark case at the U S Supreme Court. Sheriff Mack's case was based on the Tenth Amendment, States Rights and local sovereignty. Sheriff Mack said that the Federal Government could not tell him what to do; that they were not his boss. The Supreme Court agreed with him.

Since that ruling Mack has written seven books and appeared at over 120 Tea Party rallies nationwide. Sheriff Mack has fought for civil rights from Hawaii to Bangor, Maine and has now traveled to all 50 states in his battle for liberty. He is the Founder and President of the Constitutional Sheriffs and Peace Officers Association (CSPOA) and is on the Board of Directors for Oath Keepers.

Some of Sheriff Mack's honors and awards include:

- Samuel Adams Leadership Award (Local Sovereignty Coalition)
- Elected Official of the Year 1994 (NM/AZ Coalition of Counties)
- "Cicero" Award (Firearms Industry of America)
- Inducted into the NRA Hall of Fame
- Is the only person in American history to receive the highest honors for public officials from The Second Amendment Foundation, Gun Owners of America, and the NRA.
- The Second Amendment March in Washington DC of 2010 gave him the "American Patriot" award.
- Received the "Heroes Don't Wear Capes" Award from the San Marcos (Texas) Area Republicans (SMART).

In the media, Sheriff Mack was a regular guest on Freedom Watch with Judge Napolitano and has appeared on CNN, Court TV, Nightline, Hardball, Univision, Telemundo, Russia Today, Good Morning America, FOX News, Showtime's American Candidate, and over 1500 radio shows worldwide.

To order books or schedule Richard Mack to speak at an upcoming event, please contact him:

www.CSPOA.org

602-268-9268

P.O. Box 567, Higley, AZ 85236